TO THE MOTHER OF THE WORD

masterpiece of the Blessed Trinity

the
MOTHER

The Newman Press——Westminster, Maryland, 1953

O F   G O D

by M.-M. Philipon, O.P., M.S.T.

Translated by Rev. John A. Otto, Ph.D.
St. Ambrose College, Davenport, Iowa

NIHIL OBSTAT: Edward A. Cerny, S.S., D.D., Censor librorum

IMPRIMATUR: Most Reverend Francis P. Keough, D.D., Archbishop of Baltimore

April 16, 1953

The nihil obstat and imprimatur are official declarations that a book or pamphlet is free of doctrinal and moral error. No implication is contained therein that those who have granted the nihil obstat and imprimatur agree with the opinions expressed.

Library of Congress Catalog Card Number: 53-7492

FROM THE TRANSLATOR

There are many books on Mary, some old, some new, all welcome. In our day, the definition of the dogma of the Assumption has occasioned a great number of scholarly studies on Mary, as well as more popular works. Father Philipon's modest contribution is distinctive, perhaps, for its happy blending of solid content with wide appeal, of doctrine with devotion. This would seem to be its recommendation—both head and heart are well instructed.

J. A. O.

St. Ambrose College
Davenport, Iowa
Feast of the Immaculate Conception, 1952

Contents

one
INTRODUCTION TO THE MYSTERY OF MARY 3

two
THE DESTINY OF A WOMAN   12
  1 The Scriptural Perspectives 13
  2 The New Eve 15
  3 Mother, All Mother 17

three
THE IMMACULATE   20
  1 "She Shall Crush Thy Head" 20
  2 The "Almah" of Isaias 21
  3 The Woman Without Sin 22
  4 "Full of Grace" 25
  5 The Virgin Most Faithful 28

four
A WOMAN FROM OUR MIDST   31
  1 Daughter of Israel 31
  2 The Mother of the Messias 34
  3 The Mother of Jesus 37
  4 The Virgin-Mother and the Child-God 40
  5 The Wife of the Carpenter 45
  6 The Wedding at Cana 47

five
A MOTHERHOOD'S RANSOM   49
  1 The Drama of Our Redemption 50
  2 A Mother's Expiation 51

3   A Mother's Merits   56
4   A Mother's Sacrifice   60
5   A Mother's Ransom   62
6   The Coredemptress of the World   64

six
SHE WHO KEEPS WATCH OVER THE
CHURCH   68
1   Nurturing the Infant Church   70
2   "Suppliant Omnipotence"   72
3   The "Aqueduct" of All Graces   75
4   "More Mother than Queen"   78

seven
GOD'S MASTERPIECE   81
1   The Primacy of Christ   81
2   Our Predestination in Mary   83
3   The Glory of Divine Motherhood   84
4   Fullness of Grace   87
5   Fullness of Knowledge   91
6   Fullness of Power   93
7   Fullness of Glory   95
8   Mediatress Before the Blessed Trinity   98

eight
HOW THE CHURCH REGARDS MARY   101
1   Prophecies, Figures, and Symbols   101
2   Virginal Purity   104
3   Divine Motherhood   106
4   Sorrowful Compassion   109
5   Eternal Glory   112
6   The Cult of Mary   113

nine
"BEHOLD THY MOTHER!"   116
1   Spiritual Motherhood   117
2   Life in Mary   120

ten
TO MY MOTHER: MARY   126

THEOLOGICAL NOTES

I   The Divine Motherhood, the Keystone of Marian Theology   129

II   Regarding a Scientific Order for Mariology   132

III   Marian Axioms   134

IV   The New Eve   136

V   The Dogma of the Immaculate Conception and Its Consequences   137

VI   Mary's Incomparable Fullness of Grace   138

VII   The Primary Importance of the Fiat of the Incarnation   140

VIII   The Divine Motherhood and the Hypostatic Order   143

IX   Mary's Participation in the Mystery of Redemption   145

X   The Predestination of Mary   148

XI   The Rosary, the Embodiment of Devotion to Mary   150

INDEX

151

one

Introduction to the Mystery of Mary

*The divine motherhood is the ulti-
mate source of all Mary's greatness.*

Mary is the great wonderwork of God, the miracle
of miracles. She is at the summit of all created greatness. Only the inaccessible Trinity is above her, the
Father, Son, and Spirit of Love living in eternal union,
each of the three divine Persons possessing the fullness of divinity. In the unfathomable depths of the
Blessed Trinity lies concealed the unending cycle of
divine activity which issues forth in the generation
of the Word and the spiration of eternal Love. In
God all is light and love and eternal gladness. Millions upon millions of worlds could neither increase
nor diminish, not even by one particle, the glory and
the happiness of the indivisible and most Blessed
Trinity, the source of all good, the Alpha and Omega
of all that is.

The Word Incarnate, also, is infinitely above His
Mother. He is equal to His Father in divinity, in
power, in immensity, and in the eternity of His dura-
tion. He is like unto the Father in all things except

3

His divine Person, which is infinitely distinct from that of the Father and that of their mutual Spirit of Love. He came among men as their Saviour without ceasing to be God.

But the most divine Trinity and Christ excepted, Mary stands above all beings in the universe. Though, like us, a mere creature, she was elevated by divine wisdom and predilection to the supreme dignity of Mother of God. The divine motherhood puts her in a world apart, joining her by its end result to the hypostatic union and conferring upon the Mother of the Word the entire series of graces and inalienable privileges which make her the incomparable master-piece of God.

Mary, then, is the Mother of the Word, the Mother of God. Through this most wonderful destiny she is forever privileged to enjoy an unprecedented intimacy with each of the three divine Persons, being associated with the Father through having begotten the same Son, with the Word at every step of His redemptive work, and with the Holy Spirit in His mission as sanctifier of souls. The foundation for this entire mystery of Mary lies in her divine mother-hood,[1] and in studying Mary we must never for a moment lose sight of this unparalleled privilege of divine motherhood. It is the focal point of all aspects of Mary and the ultimate ground for all the perfec-tions and prerogatives of the Mother of Christ.

Indeed, in the beatific vision three things will make up the principal source of happiness for the elect: the simplicity of the divine nature, which is not divided in being communicated to the Trinity; the incarna-tion of the Word, which wrought in a truly wonder-

[1] See Theological Note I, p. 129.

ful manner the redemption of the world; and the divine motherhood of Mary, which through the motherhood of grace extends to all the elect. Thus, from the heights the primacy of the divine motherhood sheds clear light upon the entire mystery of Mary.

Everything in Mary stems from her divine motherhood, either by way of preparation for it, or as concomitant with it, or in consequence of it, the whole mystery thus preserving an indestructible unity. She is immaculate in order to become a living temple, worthy of the Word. Though a mother, she remains a virgin in order to dedicate her motherhood entirely to her Son. She is full of grace so as to receive the Word in her womb and to accomplish her mission as the Mother of all members of Christ's mystical body. Of its very nature her position as the Mother of God associates her with the sufferings and the glory of her Son, thereby making her the Coredemptress of the world and the Distributress of all graces.

Hence, everything in Mary is linked to her divine motherhood, whether it be the Immaculate Conception, her perpetual virginity, her fullness of grace, or her coredemption of the world. Linked with it, also, is the fact that now, after her life on earth in which together with Christ she merited all the graces of salvation, she dwells in the fullness of glory worthy of the Mother of God and her intercession with her Son is all-powerful. Lastly, her role as the Mediatress of all grace, in which is summed up her whole life and work both on earth and in heaven, accrues to her in consequence of being the Mother of the one Mediator of the world. On our part, the veneration we offer to Mary is also connected with her motherhood, for, wholly motivated as it is by filial affection, it is but the response of our hearts to her as the Mother of God and of men.

Like all scientific knowledge, the scientific study of Mary must be based strictly on reality. Furthermore, every science must be based on some first principle, and from the unity of its highest principle comes the unity of a science. In the study of Mary, the divine motherhood occupies the universal and architectonic role of a first principle upon which the whole science of Mary is based. Connected with this first principle is the principle of association, not by a *de jure* or a priori and necessary connection, but simply as fact— that is, in virtue of the free dispensations of divine providence. The divine motherhood, in other words, is not something in the abstract, but was so conceived and ordained by Providence as to place it against a very definite background, namely, the concrete and historical background relating to the incarnation of the Word.

First and foremost, then, Mary is the Mother of a Saviour-God, of a God who is the Redeemer. That is her essential definition, precisely as Mary. That, too, is how the chants of the liturgy address her: *Mater Salvatoris,* Mother of the Saviour, and *Alma Redemptoris Mater,* fair Mother of the Redeemer. God has associated her with the entire work of His Son in the role of Mother of God and of men. Her motherhood, divine in its essence, became through superabundance a motherhood that is coredemptive of all members of the mystical body, whose head is Christ. Motherhood that is divine and motherhood that is coredemptive: these are the two fundamental principles, one subordinated to the other, that determine the whole inner structure of the science of Mary.[2] Upon these two principles, moreover, depend all the axioms by which Mariology is guided, namely:

1 the axiom of fittingness (Latin: *convenientia*), which postulates for Mary all the graces and privileges considered reasonably necessary to accomplish her twofold mission as Mother of God and of men;

2 the axiom of conformity with Christ, which means that Mary's likeness to Christ is of the highest order, so that she approaches in excellence Christ Himself; this axiom is founded on the profound analogy that exists between the mystery of the one and the mystery of the other, mysteries that are essentially correlative, being, in a way, like double stars of the heavens with their reciprocal movements;

3 the axiom of excellence, which permits us to attribute to Mary, in the highest degree, *in summo*, all the perfections and helps that she needed;

4 lastly, the axiom of transcendence, which authorizes us to say that Mary herself received in the fullest measure all the graces and supernatural favors accorded to other saints through her mediation and fullness of superabundant grace.[3]

The foundation and explanation of all these axioms is to be found in Mary's office as Coredemptress,

[2] See Theological Note II, p. 132.
[3] See Theological Note III, p. 134.

and especially in her sublime mission as the Mother of a Saviour-God. All of them, obviously, must be applied with discretion, taking account of Mary's condition as a creature, of the limitations of her human nature, of her role as a woman, and of her life of faith. That is to say, we must resist every temptation to attribute to Mary while yet on earth the state of existence proper to angels and the blessed. To fail in this is only to fall victim to the vagaries of one's imagination. Besides, the Virgin of truth is not served by fallacious eulogies.

Every period in the history of the Church has its own particular way of considering the mystery of Mary. After Pentecost the Apostles venerated her as the Mother of Jesus. At the time of the great Christological heresies, and especially at the Council of Ephesus, the Catholic faith affirmed enthusiastically its infallible belief in her title of Mother of God, that is, the title "Theotokos." Later, from one century to the next, the study of Mary produced an ever-deepening understanding of her mystery. Her inviolate virginity was seen as the first fruits of that eminent holiness and immaculate purity which were destined to shine forth in the dogma of the Immaculate Conception. Gradually, in spite of obstacles from Protestantism and Jansenism, true devotion to Mary moved irresistibly forward and, in one form or another, spread throughout the entire Christian world. And today our people desire more than ever to live in Mary.

At this point we may well note that two fundamental traits characterize contemporary devotion to Mary. In the first place, we want to see Mary, not as one lost in ecstasy and far removed from us by her inaccessible greatness, but as a mother who is very near to us. We like to see her as one who, though being the Mother of God, was not spared the toil of household duties or such trials and difficulties of daily life as each of us encounters. Nothing reveals this modern attitude better than the realistic reflections of St. Thérèse of Lisieux. "What does me good when I think of the Holy Family," she wrote, "is to imagine them as leading a very ordinary life. . . . Everything in their life was just like ours." [4] A few days later she wrote: "The Blessed Virgin is too often depicted as one who is so unapproachable. Instead, we ought to represent her as one we can imitate by practicing hidden virtues. We ought to make clear that she lived by faith as we must, and that the proofs of this are found in the gospel itself." [5] With the Little Flower of Lisieux we, too, like to think of the Mother of God as one whose life on earth was much like that of the women we know.

There is a second trait that characterizes the contemporary attitude toward the mystery of Mary. What I mean is that today we want a robust Christianity, and in the Virgin Mary we want to find, not a dainty and delicate young woman who was ever so "pious," but rather, if one may use the term, a warrior virgin, one who was committed heart and soul to the work of the Redemption. Thus, it is not surprising that the question which dominates present-day Marian study is the one relating to her title of Coredemptress of the world, which is the foundation for her role as universal Mediatress.

The chapters that follow are an attempt to produce

[4] *Novissima verba*, Aug. 20, 1897.
[5] *Ibid.*, Aug. 23, 1897.

a synthesis of the science of Mary. Our efforts have been prompted by the questions of the moment; but we have not overlooked the more fundamental need of putting each aspect of the mystery of Mary in the place where it belongs in relation to the total conception. In general, the great need of our day is the work of synthesizing. It is, of course, always rash to attempt a synthesis as long as basic questions are still in dispute. In any event, however, one must always go back to the directive principles of a science, for whatever value or fruitfulness there may be in new theories is the result of having kept the basic principles under constant scrutiny. These alone can give coherence to a body of isolated certitudes or probabilities.

Where can we find the correct understanding to serve as a reliable introduction to the mystery of Mary? To begin with, we must put aside every subjective and a priori conception. The true perspectives of Mary are the scriptural perspectives. In the light of divine revelation a wonderful continuity links together all the aspects of this mystery, from Genesis to the Apocalypse, from the first prophetic utterance following the Fall to the splendors of glory in heaven. The gospel remains as always the foremost revelation of this mystery, for through the insights provided by the Incarnation the true character of Mary is placed in the boldest relief.

In our study of the mystery of Mary we have, in the first place, followed the successive steps of its providential development both in the course of history and in the mind and soul of Mary. Next, we have attempted to set forth, in brief survey, the whole train of graces and privileges surrounding the divine motherhood, showing how all of them derive from this fundamental mystery. Lastly, in the study of a mystery so intimately related to the very essence of Christianity, we deemed it necessary to connect these considerations of ours with the great tradition of the Church and with her way of contemplating Mary; for from the Church's approach follows, spontaneously, a filial veneration of her who is the Mother of God and our Mother.

two

The Destiny of a Woman

The new Eve.

Mary occupies a central place in the very heart of Christianity. Without her there would be no Christ. If one eliminated the sacred page that reveals to us the incarnation of the Word following the pronouncement of Mary's fiat, the gospel would lose its whole meaning and Holy Writ remain a closed book.

Indeed, Mary's name is inscribed at the center of all the mysteries of our faith. In the Creed she alone among creatures is mentioned as having had an essential role in the work of redemption. The eternal Word, true God and true man, the light of light, consubstantial with and equal to God, came down from heaven only through the mediation of Mary. In the words of the Credo of the Mass: *Et incarnatus est de Spiritu Sancto, ex Maria Virgine, et homo factus est* —"And He was made flesh by the Holy Spirit, of the Virgin Mary, and was made man." Or, as St. John has it, "And the Word was made flesh, and dwelt among us," [1] but only through Mary. We have here a most fundamental revelation regarding the destiny of this daughter of the earth who became the Mother of the eternal God. The greatest event in the history of the world is thus forever linked with her life in a most intimate manner. God willed to accomplish all His promises of salvation through her and in her. For this reason, in order to penetrate the mystery of Mary one must always approach it by way of the Incarnation.

I THE SCRIPTURAL PERSPECTIVES

It would be taking a singularly diminished view of the mystery of Mary if we considered it by itself, in isolation. The fact is that the stupendous destiny of this woman unfolds itself against the vast horizons of the Redemption. Hence the Church likes to contemplate the Mother of God and of men in the grand and tragic setting following the Fall, for these scriptural perspectives shed God's own clear light upon the universal role of the Coredemptress of the world.

Thus, alongside the Saviour, of whom they had glimpses, the prophets will always find this mysterious woman; and her image, as it were, will haunt their mind and memory. In the plan of divine requital, as in the scene of the Fall, the first protagonist whom the serpent of hell will face is the Woman. Through all the ages a struggle without respite and

[1] John 1:14. (Scriptural references in this volume are from the Douay Version for the Old Testament, and, for the New Testament, from the Confraternity of Christian Doctrine Edition; Paterson, New Jersey: St. Anthony Guild Press, 1941.—Translator's note.)

without mercy, a duel to the death, will be waged between the race of this woman on the one hand and the followers of Satan on the other. God Himself declared: "I will put enmities between thee and the woman, and thy seed and her seed." [2] At the culminating and decisive moment of the struggle the Son of the Woman, the fruit of her womb, will triumph over the serpent; and the Woman herself, in cooperation with her Son, will play an essential part in the final victory.

The entire Messianic message of succeeding ages is already contained in principle in this sublime promise of the proto-evangel. Henceforth, despite all the catastrophes of the ages to come, there will be lodged in the heart of sinful humanity a hope that nothing can erase, and men will look with confidence to this most extraordinary woman. What a far cry this divinely inspired picture of Mary from those representations which show her with the mawkish smiles and languorous airs that are only all too familiar. Such representations are veritable caricatures of her who was par excellence the valiant woman, the virgin who inspired terror in the demon and is more feared by him than an army in battle array. The God of Holy Writ Himself shows her to us as committed with all her heart to the formidable struggle between good and evil, a struggle which is only the unfolding of the eternal drama and pivotal tragedy of the world. The Mother of Christ is this same woman of Genesis, dedicated unremittingly to the work of the Redemption, the woman whom the Apocalypse will point out to us as still in the throes of childbirth until the number of the elect is fulfilled.

[2] Genesis 3:15.

Such are the true perspectives of the mystery of Mary as drawn by divine revelation. What they show us is, not a fragile young woman, too sweet and delicate for arduous combat, but a warrior virgin, the foremost soldier in the army of Christ, the Coredemptress of the world.

2 THE NEW EVE

From her earliest beginnings the Church was fully aware of the universal role of Mary, of her association with the new Adam in the capacity of the new Eve, so as to repair with Him the spiritual ruin inflicted upon humanity by the unfaithfulness of the first pair. It was clearly understood, that is, that Christ and His Mother constitute, so to speak, a Saviour-group. Christian tradition was always to remain faithful to this original inspiration which, in our own day, has been so thoroughly elucidated through the famous principle of association, a principle that is the foundation of all modern Mariological study. In the economy of redemption the new Eve is ever associated with the new Adam in the capacity of a helper like unto Himself, according to the celebrated phrase of St. Albert.[3]

According to the plan of divine redress, therefore, human nature in its entirety, both man and woman, will contribute to the work of salvation, even as both man and woman had been implicated in the Fall. All that ministered to our ruin will be used to bring about our restoration, each sex according to its providential mission: Christ as the head, Mary as associate and mother. This divine response to our ruin is truly sublime in its conception. The new Adam is God, the

[3] See Theological Note IV, p. 136.

new Eve is the Mother of God. Men are no longer just sons of Adam, but true children of God, conformed to the image of the only-begotten Son of the Father; they are living members of the Word Incarnate, called to be perfected, through Him, in the unity of the Trinity.[4]

Associated with the new Adam will be the new Eve. She will be the confidante of all His plans bearing on the Redemption. Thus, from the first pages of Genesis to the ultimate perspective of the state of glory, the Mother and the Son appear together, as two beings predestined to the same task, having in common all their thoughts, all their wishes, all their merits, all the moral value of their life of expiation and redemption, working together at the same task of salvation, even as the first man and the first woman had brought about one and the same universal ruin.

Indeed, Sacred Scripture never separates them. Mary is already present on the occasion of the first Messianic prophecy in Genesis. She is the virgin of Isaias who bears in her womb the Emmanuel. She is present to give her fiat at the decisive moment of the Incarnation, which was to bring about our redemption. Mary is always there. She is present at all the mysteries of Jesus' infancy and childhood: at Ain-Karem[5] to sanctify the Precursor through the presence of Him who lay hidden in her womb; at Bethlehem

[4] See John 17:23.

[5] The town in which Zachary and Elizabeth made their home is not named by St. Luke, but a tradition going back to the fifth century identifies it with the modern Ain-Karem, about four miles southwest of Jerusalem. Cf. Giuseppe Ricciotti, *The Life of Christ,* p. 220 (English trans. by Alba I. Zizzamia, Milwaukee, The Bruce Publishing Co., 1947).—Translator's note.

to present the Saviour to the world; at the Temple to
offer Him to His Father and to show the Messias to
the faithful among His own people as "a light of
revelation to the Gentiles, and a glory for His people
Israel." [6] One can apply to all the mysteries of Christ
the remark of the Evangelist apropos of the wedding
at Cana, namely: "And the mother of Jesus was
there." [7] She is indeed wherever her Son is found:
in Egypt, at Nazareth, at the foot of the Cross, at
Pentecost; and now, too, she is there, there in heaven,
nearer to Him than ever, united with Him in His
prayer as the Christ and in His eternal triumph.

3   MOTHER, ALL MOTHER

The wonder of wonders is that in Mary God combined all the vocations of woman; she is virgin,
spouse, and mother. Deep down in herself every woman remains, first and last, a mother. Everything in
her is ordained toward motherhood: her body, her
soul, her powers of understanding, her capacity for
affection, her aptitudes, and her inexhaustible devotion. Yes, deep in every woman lies the heart of a
mother.

Mary was not exempt from these basic laws of a
woman's nature. On the contrary, in her this highest
calling of woman was realized to the utmost. She was
essentially mother, Mother of God and of men. She
was *tota mater,* all mother. This is how Jesus Himself
referred to her from the Cross: *Ecce mater tua—*
"Behold thy mother," [8] thereby indicating that the

[6] Luke 2:32.
[7] John 2:1.
[8] John 19:27.

role of mother comprises the whole essence of the mystery of Mary.

Such, then, was the unique destiny of this woman of our race, in appearance just like the women of our acquaintance, but in reality the Mother of God in the flesh and the Mother of all men in Christ. Everything in her derives from her divine motherhood which puts her at the summit of creation and raises her up to the very confines of divinity, so as to bring her within the hypostatic order—not indeed like Christ (that is, by her very nature), but through the living and uncreated Term produced by the life-giving activity in her body. Mother of a Saviour-God, associated with Him in His entire work of ransom, she accompanied Him in the twofold phase of His saving mediation, that is to say, in the acquisition of all graces and in the distribution of all benefits of the Redemption.

In the light of what has been said we are now prepared to summarize and ponder the unique place of Mary in the economy of salvation. First, it should be clearly understood that the merciful Trinity is and remains forever the primordial and life-giving source of all that is. Secondly, on the Cross the Word Incarnate wrought in His own Person the redemption of the world, and through His Church He leads back to "the bosom of the Father" [9] those He has redeemed. But Christ, in turn, willed to associate His Mother with all His work as mediator. Accordingly, He made her the Coredemptress of the world and the repository of all the graces of the Trinity. As on the one hand,

[9] John 1:18.

therefore, no one comes to the Father but through the Son,[10] so on the other no one comes to Christ but through His Mother.[11] Such is the immutable will of God. All He gives He has willed to give through Mary.[12]

[10] See John 14:7.

[11] "Except through Mary, such being the will of God . . . so that even as no one can come to the Father, the Most High, except through the Son, so one can scarcely come to Christ except through His Mother" (Leo XIII, *Octobri mense*, Sept. 22, 1891).

[12] "Such is His will, that all we have He wanted us to have through Mary" (St. Bernard, *In Nativitate B.V.M., P.L.* 183,441).

three

The Immaculate

"Thou art all fair . . ."

From all eternity Mary was predestined by God to become the Mother of His Son and the Mother of men. As such, God in His divine liberality could hardly have failed to endow her richly with all the graces and privileges necessary for her most extraordinary mission. In order to be a worthy Mother of God, capable of sustained and relentless combat against all forces of evil, her soul had to shine forth in a luster without spot or stain. Accordingly, the radiant and resplendent Trinity decreed to make Mary Its immaculate masterpiece.

I "SHE SHALL CRUSH THY HEAD"

Already in the very beginnings of salvation foreshadowed by the earliest prophetic utterances, God gave mankind a glimpse of the triumphant purity of this woman who was chosen to be victorious over the serpent of hell. God's curse fell, inexorable, upon sinful humanity, but in vain will the tempter try to attack her, in vain will he lie in wait for her heel. She will remain invulnerable to all the venomous

stings of Satan. It is she, instead, who will crush his
head with the sovereign and serene power of the Virgin beyond all reach of sin.

Thus, this first Messianic prophecy proclaims her
brilliant victory. No doubt, by every fiber of her flesh
she belongs to the sinful race of Adam. She, too, is a
daughter of Eve. But through an unprecedented gift
of God she was totally exempt from the moral conta-
gion which since the Fall infects all human nature.
From the first she appears resplendent with purity,
dominant over evil—in a word, immaculate.

2 THE "ALMAH" OF ISAIAS

The greatest of the prophets, Isaias, had a prophetic
vision of the virgin who was to bring forth the
Emmanuel, and he saw her clothed in the brightness
of inviolable purity. It was, however, a corrupt and
troubled period of Jewish history that Isaias witnessed. The rule of Achaz was a reign of unbelief, in
which sin and wickedness in general reached convul-
sive proportions. Yet the moments of greatest desper-
ation are the moments of God. The Almighty, faithful to His promises, was about to give the house of
David an unprecedented sign. Notwithstanding its
present decay, the Messias was destined to be born of
it. As predicted in Isaias, "There shall come forth a
rod out of the root of Jesse, and a flower shall rise up
out of his root. And the spirit of the Lord shall rest
upon him." [1] Such was the promise that would be fulfilled.

With this promise went a most remarkable and
unexpected sign, one that would announce the Deliv-

[1] Isaias 11:1-2.

erer of Israel. As formerly at the Fall, so now again
we find a woman closely associated with the Saviour
in His entire work of salvation, a woman forever a
virgin. The Prophet designates her with a word that
defies translation, a word that connotes at once her
youth and her virginity. It is the word "almah," which
means a young woman who has not known man and
is resolved never to know him. She is none other than
the future Mother of the Messias, of the Emmanuel,
the "God with us." In the words of Isaias, "Hear ye,
therefore, O house of David . . . the Lord himself
shall give you a sign. Behold a virgin shall conceive,
and bear a son, and his name shall be called Emmanuel." [2]

This second Messianic and Marian prophecy proclaims a marvel so unique as to fill us with far more
wonder and astonishment than all the miracles of the
Old Testament up to that moment. Motherhood that
is both virginal and divine is promised to a daughter
of Israel. This bright vision heralding a virgin-mother
sheds the clearest light on the character of this immaculate woman, always inseparable from her Son.

3 THE WOMAN WITHOUT SIN

In the Gospels, these foreshadowings of the Old Testament will be found enhanced so as to shine forth in
all their splendor. The purity of the Immaculate will
continue to be ordered to her divine motherhood.
Indeed, it is hardly conceivable that the Son of God
should have tolerated the dishonor, one might say, of
having a mother whom sin had touched. He owed it
to Himself, in a manner of speaking, to preserve her

[2] Isaias 7: 13-14.

from all evil in a more profound and more sublime manner than is true of other creatures. He did so with divine magnificence, bestowing on her the unique privilege of being conceived immaculate, a privilege that adorns her like a royal diadem, the first fruits of His blood of redemption.

Christ, it is true, died for all men, but most of all He offered up His life for His Mother, so that she might be the most beautiful of the redeemed, intact and invulnerable. She was not freed, like us, but *preserved* from sin before contracting it, at the very moment when the Blessed Trinity created her immortal soul and joined it with her body. The effect of this privilege was to make her womanly body even more pure than an angel, and to render her maidenhood more refulgent with divine beauty than the splendor of an angel. So great was the divine resplendence in her that one finds it difficult, if not impossible, to imagine how such transcendent purity could be possessed by any being other than God. And, in fact, only the Word Incarnate excels His Mother, by reason of His being infinitely removed from all evil.

Yet, her pre-eminence notwithstanding, the Immaculate remains a member of our race. She is, in fact, the honor and the glory of her sex, the foremost among the redeemed, the masterwork wrought by the Redemption. Through the Immaculate Conception she regained the wonderful harmony human nature possessed before the Fall. So profusely did God enrich her with His divine grace that it was morally impossible for her to fall into sin of any kind. In her there was never the slightest trace of sin, no unruly desire or inclination; in her flesh, no seat of corruption; in her soul, no faintheartedness.

Furthermore, her understanding was so endowed with perfect rectitude that she could not deviate from truth. Her keen sensibilities possessed a genuinely feminine quality that has never been matched by any other woman, yet their slightest movements were always perfectly regulated and ordered to God and to what was good. Never has there been a creature more virgin, more pure, more tender, more composed. The beauty of her body reflected the divine purity of her soul. In all truth, Mary was the ideal woman, harmonizing in herself to a degree never realized before or since, all the riches of nature and grace. By her purity alone, not to mention her other merits, she was already worthy to become one day the Mother of God. She is the only creature of our race who never sinned.

To be sure, her impeccability was not like that of the Word who dwelled among men in His divine Person. Mary was impeccable in the manner of a simple creature, but in the highest degree possible to one who still lives by faith and is not yet in the state of vision in heaven. On earth her soul was flooded with such fullness of divine light and such superabundance of grace that from her very first years she lived amid the highest reaches of the transforming mystical union. Each of her deliberate acts, therefore, was performed under a special impulse from the Holy Spirit, without the possibility of any deviation from the path of perfection.

Consequently, there was never the least venial sin in her, nor even the slightest imperfection. Speaking of Mary, St. Augustine declared that where there is question of sin, he did not wish her to be included.[3]

[3] See *De Natura et Gratia*, Chap. 36.

The Church has made this sentiment her own. In her liturgy she chants as follows: "Thou art all fair, O Mary, and the stain of original sin was never in thee."[4] It is this same Mary who came back to earth in France to tell us her incommunicable name. "I am the Immaculate," she said. Truly, Mary alone among all women is the woman without sin.[5]

4 "FULL OF GRACE"

We have been considering the negative aspect of the mystery of the Immaculate, the only human being who was without stain in the sight of God. But in contemplating the negative aspect we must not overlook the positive side of the fullness of grace that was hers. For by this privilege Mary from the very first moment of her existence was raised to a degree of holiness with which the combined holiness of all the angels and saints cannot compare. Thus at the first instant of her life she was already far above all creatures of the universe.

The soul of the Immaculate was endowed with incomparable divine splendor. It was, so to speak, crystal pure. From the beginning of her life, therefore, Mary was the one most beloved of God, most lavished with grace, most pleasing in His sight. If, according to St. Catherine of Siena, the glimpse of an immortal soul in the state of friendship with God would be enough to make one die, what shall we say of the soul of Mary, which is the delight of God and the paradise, as it were, of the Blessed Trinity? A more recent testimony along this line comes from

[4] "Tota pulchra es, Maria, et macula originalis non est in te."
[5] See Theological Note V, p. 137.

Pope Pius IX. Contemplating the beauty of the soul of the Immaculate on the occasion when he proclaimed the dogma of the Immaculate Conception, he was so overwhelmed with divine illumination that but for a special grace he should, as he later affirmed, have died of joy and happiness.

It is by applying the basic and strictly authentic principles governing the theology of grace that we get some notion, imperfect though it be, of the grandeur and holiness possessed by Mary through the privilege that made her the Immaculate. Thus, even before she was old enough to understand what great mystery surrounded her, her whole being was oriented toward the hypostatic order, an order that is infinitely above the order of grace and constitutes the summit and center of attraction of her entire mystery. Hence, from the first moment of her existence Mary is found in the supernatural order, her soul overflowing, as it were, with torrents of divine grace. Indeed, next to Christ, the Immaculate is the masterpiece of God.

In Mary, moreover, all the marvelous effects of sanctifying grace were realized to a degree that the human mind cannot fully comprehend. Her whole being was made divine through grace to such an extent that she is the created image that most nearly resembles the Blessed Trinity. She received the grace of adoption, and of this grace she, rather than Christ, is the prototype for all creatures called to receive it, since Christ is the Son of God by nature, not by adoption. The indwelling of the three divine Persons in the innermost depths of her soul made her the most beautiful living temple of the Trinity that ever was or shall be.

Furthermore, in Mary all these marvelous gifts of grace lay not barren, but flowered forth in most wonderful godlike deeds and works, in which she manifested the perfect practice of all virtues, both acquired and infused. All her actions, in fact, were under the constant direction and movement of the gifts of the Holy Spirit, and this on the highest level of the transforming union. For this reason her merit was beyond measure by any standards we know, and it was always increasing and making her ready by leaps and bounds, one might say, for the supreme and wholly gratuitous dignity of the divine motherhood; and in due time, on the day of her Assumption, it would at last bring about her total transformation in God through the light of His glory.

If it were not outside the scope of this book, this would be the place, first, to review the principles governing growth and progress in the practice of the virtues and the exercise of the gifts of the Holy Spirit; and, secondly, to make application of these principles to Mary, but in the highest degree, *in summo,* according to the principle laid down by St. Albert the Great. We should find in Mary a faith illuminated by the gifts of understanding, of knowledge, and especially of wisdom; we should find an unconquerable hope, so that she was always serene and untroubled interiorly. Neither the anxieties attendant upon the childhood of Jesus nor the apparent failure of Golgotha nor the first persecutions against the infant Church could undermine her deep inward peace of soul.

We should find, too, a life of devotion, of prayer, of praise and glory unto God; a keen and responsive charity toward everyone; a justice tempered by the gift of piety. Above all we should find in Mary a love without reservation, without limit or restriction, making her ever more docile to the slightest impulses of the Spirit of God so that she might best serve the work of redemption. All this grandeur Mary possessed without fanfare, without drawing attention to herself, thereby imitating the hidden and immutable God, whose almighty power lies calm and serene over the universe, sustaining the world He created through it.

Externally, there was nothing about Mary that would have made one suspect the fullness of grace that was hers, a fullness so complete as to blind the vision of even the pure spirits, the angels. We must not try to measure her greatness in terms of quantity, for it is not something that can be put into mathematical formulas. Mary's grandeur lies beyond the order of quantity; it lies in the realm of the purely spiritual. Through the fullness of grace, her soul was introduced into the realm of God's intimate life, in which she participates in the highest degree possible for a creature. For this reason she is the perfect model of all virtues, possessing all to a pre-eminent degree, with sovereign mastery over all passions and emotions, and with perfect innocence of life—all these the inalienable privileges of the Immaculate.[6]

5   THE VIRGIN MOST FAITHFUL

In the soul of Jesus the measure of sanctifying grace was, from the first, consummated with a fullness that was in some way infinite and therefore incapable of increase. In Mary, on the other hand, we behold the

[6] See Theological Note VI, p. 138.

Church's perfect example of progressive spiritual growth. The grace that made her the Immaculate was only a point of departure, an initial fullness destined to grow unceasingly with every act of hers in a measure it would be rash to try to ascertain precisely. Our only criteria in the matter are the general principles governing the theology of grace. These justify the conclusion that the least of her daily actions possessed a greater meritorious, satisfactory, and impetratory value than all the merits of the Church militant combined. It is not exaggeration to say that one of Mary's smiles gave more glory to God than the testimony by blood of all the martyrs. From the time of her first deliberate acts her intercessory power was mightier to move God to compassion than that of all the angels and saints, though her acts could never equal the infinite value of the personal acts of Christ.

Each of her meritorious acts, moreover, earned for herself a higher degree of grace. That being the case, how could one determine the precise stages of an interior life mounting up to God by such rapid and extraordinary strides? Her faith, becoming progressively more luminous and penetrating, gave her an insight into the inmost being of the Deity that grew ever more comprehensive and more profound. In her, as we have said, all virtues reached a heroic degree together, constantly under the guiding impulse of a love that grew ever more pure and ever more intense, a love that was continuously inspired by the gifts of the Holy Spirit. In brief, the perfectly immaculate life of Mary was an uninterrupted going up to the immutable Blessed Trinity.

External events, however, were soon to bring her life as mere woman to a halt. She would be a mother and find herself engaged in the whole drama of the Redemption with the heart of a mother. For this she was already being prepared by the fidelity of the heart of the virgin that she was.

four

A Woman from Our Midst

Beneath most ordinary appearances a most divine life.

I   DAUGHTER OF ISRAEL

In its outward manifestations the life of Mary was similar to that of other young women of Israel. The background of her early years most likely was Jerusalem. On her mother's knees she learned to repeat the word "Adonai," the holy name of the Lord. Later, as a grown young lady, she used to go to the public well to fetch water and would return carrying the filled jar on her head, as was the custom. Moving along with light and graceful steps, she mingled with other women carrying water for their household needs. At home her day was taken up with the usual household chores. When evening came, she continued to work by the light of an oil lamp and could be heard humming one of those softly plaintive melodies so dear to all women of the Orient. All in all, a most routine existence, externally.

But in her soul, what divine splendor! The Law of the Lord set the pattern of her life, as it did for every

31

Jewish woman, in the most minute details—at home, in travel, at prayer, in her social life and on religious feasts, every moment of the day from morning to night. A true daughter of Israel, Mary observed the Law with perfect interior submission. She was a living portrait of the perfect Israelite who knew how to preserve and cherish in her heart the true spirit of Jahve.

Each day the recitation of the Shema, the great prayer for the Jewish liturgy, recalled to her the first precept of the Law, the great commandment of love. The scribes and Pharisees, it is true, had buried the inward spirit of this commandment under the trappings of legalistic observances. But Mary's soul could not be fettered by externals. How deeply she must have been impressed as she pronounced or listened to the words: "Hear, O Israel, the Lord our God is one Lord. Thou shalt love the Lord thy God with thy whole heart, and with thy whole soul, and with thy whole strength." [1] Three times daily, also, she sang the following hymn of praise to the Lord God:

Blessed be Thou, eternal Lord, our God,
Creator of heaven and of earth;
Thou art our highest hope from generation to
    generation;
Thou humblest those who exalt themselves, Thou
    judgest those who oppress;
Thou raisest up the dead.

The family meals with their religious ceremonies reminded her of the many blessings God had bestowed on His chosen people. But most of all Mary

[1] Deuteronomy 6:4-5.

was fascinated by the Temple and by the mystery of the divine presence at this center of worship for Israel. Gladly she lived her life under the shadow of the Temple of the eternal God. There her soul, pure and full of faith, was favored with abundant illuminations from on high. With other young Israelite women she took part in the sacred dances and festivities. Early in her life the wonderful destinies of Israel began to possess her soul. A true daughter of David, she understood so many things, instinctively. The Sacred Scriptures, on which she meditated continually and many passages of which she knew by heart, molded her soul according to the spirit of Jahve. The Prophets, and especially the Psalms, often came to her mind. These sacred texts struck a resonant chord deep in the youthful soul of Mary. For was it not she who occupied such a privileged position in regard to these same Scriptures—she, and He who was to be her Son? Truly, a unique position. She penetrated the meaning of the inspired books more deeply than all the doctors of Israel. Thus, quite naturally, the expectation of the Messias more and more directed the course of her interior life.

Up to this point Mary had been living in obscurity. Then, one day, an event took place which created a sensation and put the entire city of Jerusalem in commotion. Each evening at the hour of the daily sacrifice a priest entered the Holy Place of the Temple and offered incense before the Lord. At the moment when the smoke of the incense was seen rising up to God, the people, bursting forth in joyful shout, would join voices with the Levites who were singing the praises of God to the accompaniment of instruments.

On the day in question the priest named Zachary was officiating according to the order of his course. Suddenly, an angel of the Lord appeared to him and announced that, old as they were, he and his wife would have a son and call him John. This child would be "great before the Lord; he . . . shall be filled with the Holy Spirit even from his mother's womb. And many of the children of Israel he shall bring back to the Lord their God, and he himself shall go before him in the spirit and power of Elias . . . to prepare for the Lord a perfect people." [2]

Hearing this, the aged priest began to tremble. God had chosen him in his old age to father the precursor of the Messias. Almost instinctively he remembered the prophecy of Malachias: "Behold I send my angel, and he shall prepare the way before my face. And presently the Lord, whom you seek, and the angel of the testament, whom you desire, shall come to his temple. Behold he cometh, saith the Lord of hosts." [3] Clearly, the time of the Messias was at hand.

2 THE MOTHER OF THE MESSIAS

Another marvelous event soon followed—one that was to dominate the whole course of history. It took place, not in Jerusalem amid the splendors of the Temple, but in a very unpretentious home in Galilee, where a young woman was living a quiet, unnoticed life. According to the eternal plan of God, the moment of the fullness of time had come. The Father was about to give the world the highest proof of His love by sending His Son into it. In a manner of speaking,

[2] Luke 1:15-17.
[3] Malachias 3:1.

the whole Trinity was rejoicing, and the entire angelic universe was thrilled with joy in anticipation of this stupendous mystery. A messenger of the Most High was sent from heaven to a small town of Galilee called Nazareth, to a virgin betrothed to a young man named Joseph, of the house of David. And the virgin's name was Mary.

"Hail, full of grace, the Lord is with thee," said the angel as he entered her home. Completely surprised, the young woman wondered what this unusual greeting might betoken. A lowly virgin, she appeared troubled and astonished, but the angel reassured her, saying, "Do not be afraid, Mary, for thou hast found grace with God." And then the divine message is unfolded to her in striking utterances delivered in rapid succession: "Behold, thou shalt conceive in thy womb and shalt bring forth a son; and thou shalt call his name Jesus. He shall be great, and shall be called the Son of the Most High; and the Lord will give him the throne of David his father, and he shall be king over the house of Jacob forever; and of his kingdom there shall be no end."

In one act of intuitive insight, produced by a prophetic illumination surpassing that of all the revelations of the Old Testament, Mary at this moment understood all. She understood that the God of Israel had chosen her to become the Mother of the Messias. Immediately all the promises of Sacred Scripture passed before her mind in their full and unmistakable meaning. She saw clearly that what was being announced to her was the divine sonship of the Messias and His eternal reign.

One question, however, remained in her mind. As the Virgin most prudent she inquired, "How shall this happen, since I do not know man?" Again a divine illumination, as unprecedented as it was astounding, enlightened her understanding. Hers was to be a motherhood without the loss of maidenhood. Man would not have his usual part in it. This miraculous motherhood would be the exclusive work of the Most High. In the words of the angel: "The Holy Spirit shall come upon thee and the power of the Most High shall overshadow thee; and therefore the Holy One to be born shall be called the Son of God," having only God for His Father.

(Yes, Mary, far from violating your virginity, this divine motherhood would be its highest consecration. An unheard-of wonder, to be sure; but, then, "nothing shall be impossible with God." Did He not just recently make it possible for your cousin Elizabeth to conceive in her old age and thus become the mother of the Precursor?)

After this crowning revelation, all was clear. Mary understood that her motherhood would be both divine and virginal. She realized that she was holding the destiny of the world in the balance. For, would not her Son be the Saviour of the world? God Himself, one might say, was urging her to accept her role in the accomplishment of His eternal plan; and the whole world was awaiting her consent. Without hesitation and fully aware of the universal import of her act, Mary, in order to repair the harm inflicted upon the human race by the Fall, pronounced her "yes," and thereby she was forever and irrevocably committed to serving the work of the Redemption. "Behold," she said, "the handmaid of the Lord; be it done to me according to thy word." [4] With that,

[4] See Luke 1:28-38.

the angel left her. She whom he had greeted a virgin, was now the Mother of God as well.[5]

3 THE MOTHER OF JESUS

A momentous change had come over Mary, a change that transformed her whole being. Motherhood always brings about a profound psychological alteration in a woman. Her child becomes the center of her whole life. If this is true in general, how much more so when it is the Son of the Virgin and the child is God!

We can scarcely imagine the thoughts and feelings of this young Mother of God who, while continuing to be a woman from our midst, was to learn by faith, from "the bosom of the Father," [6] the mystery of her Son. From this moment her life is centered heart and soul on this child who is God, equal to the Father by His divine nature and, together with Him, the Principle from whom proceeds the Holy Spirit. Interiorly, at the summit of her soul, Mary's understanding is henceforth engaged solely in contemplating the Word Incarnate dwelling among men, yet abiding in mystery in the Father, who is the infinitely living and life-giving source of the Son's eternal generation.[7]

In the light of the Incarnation, which was accomplished in her, Mary understood clearly the whole meaning of the Old Testament. The living presence of the Word in her womb bore witness to her of the divine sonship of the Messias. The true dimensions of her motherhood began to be manifest. She became

[5] See Theological Note VII, p. 140.   [6] John 1:18.
[7] See Theological Note VIII, p. 143.

aware that she was both the Mother of the only-begotten Son of the Father and the Mother of men, the Mother, that is, of all the children of God called to become by adoption members of the family of the Trinity. She realized, in other words, that she was the Mother of the total Christ. As such, her maternal heart and mind reached out beyond space and time, into the past, present, and future, to enfold in one embrace all the sons of God, the brothers of Jesus. In doing so she was filled with wonder as she contemplated the universal extent and the indissoluble unity of the mystical body, of which she had become the Mother, having conceived by one and the same fiat both the head and the members, both the "first-born" and the "many brethren." [8] The result of her unprecedented consent was to fill her heart, instantly and forever, with the feelings and affections of a mother both toward Christ and toward all the children of God. And like a true mother, she wanted now to live only for her children.

In the days that followed, Mary could not but be pondering all these things in her heart. Prompted by the message of the angel and the inspiration of God, she went "with haste" to visit her cousin Elizabeth. As she made her way across the plains of Galilee southward to Judea and traversed the Holy Land, where almost every inch of ground evoked a sacred memory, scriptural passages came crowding in her mind, recalling the countless blessings the God of Israel had vouchsafed to His people. Enlightened by the invisible presence of the Messias in her womb, the whole array of Old Testament promises took on for her a new and deeper meaning. The ground itself

[8] Romans 8:30.

under her feet seemed to be vibrant with life, so full of joy and expectation was she.

Hardly had she arrived at the house of her cousin in the small village of Ain-Karem,[9] when she was witness to further marvelous happenings produced by God. At the approach of the Saviour in the womb of Mary, Elizabeth's child leaped in her womb. Prophetically inspired, she saluted Mary as the woman blessed above all women, chosen by God to be the Mother of the Messias. "How," she asked, "have I deserved that the mother of my Lord should come to me?" [10]

In utterances that are among those the Church treasures most highly, the humble virgin Mary, overflowing with happiness in having become the Mother of God, gave expression to the joy in her maternal heart. "He who is mighty," she replied, "has done great things for me. To Him be all glory. He has regarded the lowliness of His handmaid. He has shown might with His arm. He has exalted the lowly. Holy is His name, and for generation upon generation is His mercy. He has given help to Israel, His servant, as He spoke to our fathers, to Abraham and to his posterity forever." [11]

The full light of the Incarnation had become manifest to Mary, giving everything in her life a new meaning and bearing. All the secrets of the divine plan were revealed to her. It was she, despite her lowliness and unworthiness, whom God deigned to favor with the grace of being chosen the Mother of the Messias. She received, also, a prophetic vision of all

[9] See page 16, note 5.
[10] Luke 1:43.
[11] See Luke 1:49-55.

generations who would proclaim her blessed. Yet it was not for any merit on her part that God wrought such wonder, raising her up to the dignity of being the Mother of His Son. It was a gratuitous gift that God bestowed on her; and, indeed, the taking of flesh in her womb by the only-begotten Son of the Father, is it not the highest pledge of a mercy that has been received for all time?

Furthermore, behind the scriptural overtones, behind what might be called the millenarian phrases of the Magnificat, can be detected a new resonance. It is, in other words, all Israel which sings through Mary, but already under the inspiration of the Spirit of the Son. The Magnificat is the triumphal hymn to the incarnation of the Word. The personal canticle of the Mother of Jesus, it expresses the inmost thoughts and feelings of the Mother of God.

4 THE VIRGIN-MOTHER AND THE CHILD-GOD

Mary remained with Elizabeth about three months, ministering, as one devoted to the family, to her every need. The two cousins used the opportunity to converse about the respective destinies of their children, the one the Precursor, the other the Saviour. After the birth of John the Baptist Mary went back to Nazareth, her soul radiant with happiness in the certainty that salvation was at hand.

Joseph was overjoyed to see her again. But it was not to be long before unspeakable and unexpected anguish would grip his soul. The first signs of motherhood, evident and undeniable, began to show in Mary. To all appearances his fiancée, the most beautiful and the purest of the virgins of Nazareth, stood accused of sin. Still, Joseph did not doubt her innocence. Yet how great must have been his perplexity and bewilderment! Since he did not know where to turn, his distress was all the more excruciating. Mary could have explained everything with one word, but she preferred to be silent, trusting to God. A just man, however, as we see in the case of Joseph, will never condemn a woman without clear-cut proof of her guilt. In the present instance, two solutions offered themselves. Joseph could either denounce Mary as provided for by the Law and thus expose her to public shame, or he could secretly deposit a bill of divorce before two judges and thus give Mary her freedom. In either case it would be a definitive separation for these two souls who loved each other. Joseph finally decided to send her away as discreetly as possible. But what would happen to her then? Public defamation, that was certain; perhaps she would even be stoned to death.

As Joseph was pondering his course of action, an angel appeared to him in a dream and said: "Do not be afraid, Joseph, son of David, to take to thee Mary thy wife, for that which is begotten in her is of the Holy Spirit. And she shall bring forth a son, and thou shalt call his name Jesus; for he shall save his people from their sins." [12] This divine revelation removed all doubts from his mind and all anguish from his heart. He understood that his fiancée was the "almah" of Isaias and that in becoming a mother she remained a virgin.

In effect, the message of the angel deputed Joseph to be the legal father of Mary's Son; as His supposed

[12] Matthew 1:20-22.

father, he would name Him Jesus. In one act of
inspired insight Joseph understood all. Mary, he realized, was the Mother of the Messias! Waking from
his dream, he arose full of joy and hurried to Mary to
tell her of the vision he had had. As Mary listened,
her heart was filled with gladness. Once again she
praised God for His great mercy and in turn
recounted to Joseph the mystery of the annunciation
and of the incarnation of the Word. Blessed be God!
Such must have been their fervent sigh. Now they
would be forever united in the common task of ministering to the work of His Son and the salvation of
the world. Nothing would separate them, ever. At
the end of their conversation, drawing near each
other, they united themselves forever in an act of
consecration to God, loving each other with a love
that was always to remain virginal.

Their life at Nazareth in the next few months was
peaceful and uneventful, until Caesar Augustus is-
sued a decree ordering a census to be taken of the
whole world. God was so disposing the events of
the world that, in preparing a cradle for His Son,
the prophecy of Micheas would be fulfilled, namely:
"And thou, Bethlehem Ephrata, art a little one
among the thousands of Juda: out of thee shall he
come forth unto me that is to be the ruler in
Israel." [13]

After two or three days of travel the young couple
arrived at last in Jerusalem. In view of her condition
it had been a fatiguing journey for Mary, and at the
end of it she knew her days were about to be fulfilled. In vain did they seek lodgings in one of the
caravansaries of Bethlehem. Being poor, they found

[13] Micheas 5:2.

there was no room for them. Hence there was nothing for Mary and Joseph to do but retire to a sort of cave in the neighborhood, which served both as a shelter for people and a stable for animals. There, soon after their arrival, took place in the dead of night the miraculous birth. A manger for animals became the cradle for the Child-God. The Virgin-Mother, wrapping Him in swaddling clothes, adored Him as the Son of the eternal God. If Golgotha discomfits our reason by its tragedy, the Crib embarrasses us by its simplicity. A God in a stable, and at His side a young mother heaping Him by turns with kisses and adorations!

Not only its beginnings, but the whole mystery of the childhood of Jesus is unfolded against a background of contrasts, with alternating manifestations of common frailty and stupendous marvels, of the human and the divine. Thus, the angels come from heaven to herald the birth of the Saviour of the world, but the sign they give is "an infant wrapped in swaddling clothes." His Mother receives the simple, lowly shepherds with great joy. She listens attentively to all they say. As they recount in their simple manner the vision they saw in the night of the multitude of angels singing and glorifying Him who dwells in the highest, she marvels at God's ways, that He should make known His Son, first of all, to the lowly and the poor. Later the learned and the rich will come. Mary will receive them with the same kindness, for He came to save all men. Thus, in various ways the light of God would show men the path that leads to His Son. His very name of Jesus, given Him by Joseph at the circumcision, denotes most aptly His mission of Saviour.

We find Mary and the child next in the Temple. On the day designated by the Law for purification, Mary, accompanied by Joseph, brought the child to Jerusalem. It was a small retinue that came, but it was the occasion for the Messias to enter His Temple for the first time, and it was fitting that He should be greeted by one of the prophets. The aged Simeon, a just man who was looking for the consolation of Israel, had come by inspiration of the Holy Spirit. God had assured him that he would not die before he should see the Christ, the Anointed of the Lord. He came on the same day as Mary and Joseph. Externally, there was nothing about their arrival to distinguish them from any other poor family coming to perform the usual rites prescribed by the Law. When the ceremony was over, the aged man took the child from Mary's arms and holding Him up before him said, "Now thou dost dismiss thy servant, O Lord . . . because my eyes have seen thy salvation." [14]

Then, going beyond this personal perspective, he foretold what the coming of this child would mean for Israel and all nations. Mary and Joseph, marveling at what was said, had a new insight into the future of their Son, the glory of Israel and a revelation to the Gentiles. Doubtless, it would be centuries upon centuries before the enlightenment of His presence had spread to the ends of the earth, but the time would come when, in all truth, He would be the light of the whole world. [15]

All the while, the child seemed to be asleep. Turning to the mother, the prophet continued:

[14] Luke 2:29-30.
[15] See John 12:46.

"Behold, this child is destined for the fall and for the rise of many in Israel, and for a sign that shall be contradicted. And thy own soul a sword shall pierce . . ." [16] Already Calvary was beginning to cast its shadow over her who would be associated with the Passion and the death of her Son. A common tragic destiny united Mother and Son in a common redemptive suffering.

Wherever Jesus went His Cross followed Him. The Saviour's entire childhood will be for Mary an imperceptible yet inexorable going up to Golgotha. Bethlehem, the massacre of the Innocents, the hasty flight into Egypt and the equally hasty return to Nazareth: these are the next stages in the life of the Redeemer and the Coredemptress of the world. What is important to note in this successive unfolding of mysteries is not so much the details of the narrative as the profound meaning underlying the dramatic and tragic spectacle of a God living among men. And also to be noted is the intimate connection between the destiny of the Mother and that of the Son.

5 THE WIFE OF THE CARPENTER

Nothing could have been less extraordinary than the life of the Holy Family at Nazareth. In the eyes of the inhabitants of this delightful little town, Mary was simply the wife of the carpenter. Like the other women of the countryside, she gave all her time to her household chores. Like them, she could be seen at the public well, in the synagogue, at the market place getting provisions for her family. Living a simple life, she went and came unnoticed. Joseph meanwhile

[16] Luke 2:34-35.

earned their livelihood by working at his trade. Their Son Jesus grew and developed under their watchful care, much as any other child. No one suspected the divine grandeur of the Son of Mary. He mingled with the other children of the town and advanced in age and wisdom, but without causing astonishment. He was polite and intelligent, with a candor of soul that captivated both the neighbors and the close friends of the family. Joseph's was a model home, where life centered around the activities of a small workshop. There, unheeded, lived the God of the universe, the Mother of the Word Incarnate, and Joseph, "a just man," who surpasses all the angels and saints in holiness.[17] Thus it is that the great works of God are always prepared in silence and obscurity.

In the Gospels the life of the Holy Family is told very briefly. In the apocryphal accounts, on the other hand, the childhood of the Saviour, perhaps in response to a desire for more detail, has been overlaid with legendary particulars and fabricated miracles. By comparison, how much more striking and revealing in its very conciseness is the simple remark

[17] St. Joseph's pre-eminent holiness over that of all the angels and saints derives from his threefold mission, a mission that is second only to that of the divine motherhood, namely: (1) his role as head of the Holy Family and, by extension, his office as protector of the Church of Christ; (2) his role as spouse of the Mother of God; (3) lastly and most important of all, his role as the deputed father of the Word Incarnate, a role in which lies the highest source of his pre-eminent greatness. As the Preface of the Mass of St. Joseph declares, he was chosen to watch over "Thine only-begotten Son with fatherly care" (ut Unigenitum tuum . . . paterna vice custodiret). On this point, see Pope Leo XIII's Encyclical Quamquam pluries, Aug. 15, 1889.

of Jesus: "Did you not know that I must be about my Father's business?" [18] This is the only recorded utterance of Jesus during His first thirty years. But it is a most profound utterance, revealing by one stroke the whole mystery of Christ, namely, His divine Person and the habitual disposition of His filial soul. Mary, contemplating these words of Jesus and others of similar import, must have been inspired with the most profound insights, for "she kept all these things carefully in her heart." [19] Thus, amid the silence of Nazareth, Jesus was molding the heart and soul of the Coredemptress of the world.

6 THE WEDDING AT CANA

There is perhaps no incident in the Gospels which better illustrates the power of Mary over the heart of her Son than the wedding at Cana. The true character of the Mother of God, who lived among men like a woman from our midst, is nowhere else so clearly portrayed as in this well-known episode. The Mother of Jesus, we learn, was not a mystic who went about blindfolded, as it were, and was so absorbed in God as to be oblivious of the exigencies of human life. On the contrary, she was a most observant woman, acutely sensitive even to the smallest material needs of those around her.

On this occasion she noticed that an embarrassing moment had come in the celebration. Fully aware of the predicament, she turns discreetly to her Son— only He could save the situation. "They have no wine," she says to Him, her voice betraying her con-

[18] Luke 2:49.
[19] Luke 2:51.

cern. What an awkward circumstance for the family! They had not anticipated the sudden arrival of Nathanael accompanied by Jesus and His disciples. Yet it would hardly be proper for invited guests to take notice of the quandary. Hence Jesus replies to His Mother, "What wouldst thou have me do, woman? My hour has not yet come." On the surface it was a refusal. But Jesus really could not refuse His Mother anything; Mary knew that better than any one.

After His answer, she understood from His look and demeanor that she could proceed to bring to bear upon Him the tenderness and irresistible power of a mother. "Do whatever he tells you," she whispers to the attendants. Whereupon Jesus says to them, "Fill the jars with water." They filled them to the brim, and Jesus changed the water into wine. "This first of his signs," concludes the Evangelist, "Jesus worked at Cana of Galilee; and he manifested his glory, and his disciples believed in him." [20]

St. John, who witnessed the miracle, underlines, as of greater importance even than the miracle itself, the fact of Mary's presence when he says, "And the mother of Jesus was there." It was at the request of His Mother that the Founder of Christianity, in the presence of the Apostolic circle, who were the first fruits of the Christian community, was pleased to manifest to His newly recruited disciples His divine power as wonder-worker. The whole incident symbolizes the unique place that Mary was to occupy in His Church. Jesus alone, it is true, is the Saviour; but His Mother's intercession with Him is all-powerful, able to obtain all things.

[20] See John 2:1-12.

five

A Motherhood's Ransom

The Calvary of a mother.

Like that of Jesus, the life of Mary was one continuous act of redemptive expiation. From the moment of her fiat at the incarnation and the conception of the Redeemer in her womb, a common destiny united the Mother and the Son forever. Their intimate association extended to every moment of their life, growing ever deeper. They were united in mind and will, in the same sufferings and the same joys, all in view of the same work of redemption. Together, "by their respective merits,"[1] they saved the world.

Quite properly, therefore, does modern Mariology put emphasis on the principle of association. According to this principle, an indissoluble bond unites the Redeemer and the Coredemptress in the two distinct but complementary aspects of the economy of salvation, namely, in the *acquisition* and the *distribution* of all graces. This is the master idea governing and underlying Mariology, and it throws the greatest possible light on the actions, even the smallest, of the life of Mary and Jesus. From all eternity God associated

[1] "Amborum meritis," from the Prayer of the privileged Mass of the Rosary according to the Dominican Rite.

the new Eve with the new Adam. In this association Christ is the head of the mystical body, and His actions among men proceed according to the free determinations of a divine Person, whereas Mary's role is wholly subordinated to that of Jesus. Yet, as Mother of God and of men, her work in the economy of salvation is not less universal in extent than her Son's.

I THE DRAMA OF OUR REDEMPTION

After Jesus left His home at Nazareth, Mary's thoughts followed Him everywhere. Occasionally, also, she could be seen moving, unobtrusive, among the throngs of Galilee, who wondered at this young rabbi "mighty in work and word,"[2] performing at will the most astounding miracles. She observed how the lowly and the poor gathered around Jesus in awe and veneration, whereas the Pharisees and doctors of the Law plotted against Him. She saw that the hatred of His enemies was increasing by the day. As she meditated on the prophecy of Isaias concerning the suffering Messias, her maternal heart could not but have been filled with anguish. She understood that her Son would be put to death like a sheep led to the slaughter, and that He would die, a man of sorrows, with the wicked, carrying the burden of all the sins of the world. It was during the three years of His public life, and particularly during the last days of His Passion and death, that Mary more than ever was one in sentiment and suffering with the soul of her Son.

Thus, when the hour of redemption came, she was ready to unite herself with the supreme oblation of

[2] Luke 24:19.

Christ on the Cross. Together they were to redeem and save all. Hence, Golgotha was simultaneously the climax of the redemptive Passion of Jesus and of the coredemptive compassion of Mary. Indeed, Mary's compassion at the Cross was her highest achievement. Her own merit, it is true, could still increase after the resurrection of her Son, and her intercessory power could be further enlarged by her subsequent acts of love in the service of the infant Church. But the fact is that the Mother of Christ could not have performed a more sublime act than she performed at the moment when she consented to the immolation of her Son on the Cross. In her mission as universal Mediatress this unprecedented immolation holds the same central place as it does in the mediation of Christ. For, it was on Golgotha that the fate of the world was sealed; and the fate of each of our personal lives depends on the act of salvation there accomplished.

The best way to appreciate the true worth of Mary's coredemptive compassion is to compare it with the redemptive Passion of Christ. Christ's act was that of the head who saved His people by offering up His own life; that of Mary consisted in a mother's consent to the heroic death of her Son for the salvation of His brethren. Christ suffered in His flesh; Mary in her soul. Christ's sacrifice was that of a priest; Mary's Calvary, that of a mother.

2 A MOTHER'S EXPIATION

The highest task that fell to Christ and His Mother was the act of atonement for all the sins of the world. This concern to secure the Father's glory by making reparation for original sin and for all of our personal transgressions was a basic motivation in the psychology of the Redeemer and in that of the Coredemptress. To measure the full importance of this atonement we should need the capacity to fathom the infinite malice contained in every mortal sin, even in the least offensive—something we commit so readily, almost with a smile of indifference, but something it took the blood of a God to atone.

Jesus Himself, being God, was able to understand the malice of sin as only God can. Being God, too, He saw all the transgressions of all men, past, present, and future. This spectacle of all the sins of all men caused Him, day and night, indescribable sorrow of soul. The sweating of blood at Gethsemane is dramatic evidence of this fact. So great was His sorrow that, had He not been sustained by His Father, it would have been enough to make Him die of grief. It is understandable, then, that the desire to make reparation for this mass of sin should have been the determining motive of His incarnation. Hence, to atone for these outrages against God's majesty the Son, in an act of infinite love, offered Himself up in our stead. St. Paul, recalling Psalm 39, writes: "Therefore in coming into the world he says: 'Sacrifices and oblation thou wouldst not, but a body thou hast fitted to me . . . Then said I: Behold, I come . . . to do thy will, O God.'" [3]

If we are to comprehend the great malice of sin, we must view it in the light of the Cross. Once it was committed, only two alternatives were possible. Either sinful man had to undergo punishment com-

[3] Hebrews 10:6-7.

mensurate with strict justice, or a God had to supply atonement. To this work of expiation Christ devoted His whole being and His whole life, all that He was and all that He had, His divine Person, His grace of headship, and all of His immense sufferings. Since even the least of His actions possessed infinite value, the God-man was able to offer to the Blessed Trinity a reparation that not only equalled but infinitely outweighed the malice of all the sins of the world. One act of love from His Son become flesh gave the Father more satisfaction than the combined sins of men and the rebellious angels gave Him offense.

Jesus offered up the life of a God in our stead; the head atoned for the members. In virtue of the indissoluble bond that unites His entire mystical body, all the acts of Christ together with their infinite value are placed at our disposition. His expiation, His merit, His supplication, His adoration and praise, all are ours. Through this mystery of unity we are permitted to appear before the Father in the very character and name of the Son. For we are one with Christ through the mystery of substitution whereby we are identified with Him in the order of redemption. It was in our behalf that He atoned for guilt and made satisfaction for punishment. All His merits are ours. Through faith and love, and through the sacraments, each one of us can make them his own. Their value is infinite, for Christ's atonement, let it be repeated, infinitely surpasses the sum total of all the sins of the world. That is why every sinner, even the greatest, may approach the throne of God's mercy fully confident that he will be received. All has been forgiven.

The coredemptive action of Mary in behalf of the

mystical body was of a different sort. Her role was
essentially that of a mother. Her expiation, her merit,
her sacrificial oblation, her ransom, all were those of
a mother. Indeed, it would be a great mistake to consider Mary as a replica of Christ. Mary is not a Christ
of the feminine sex. She is a mother, the woman associated with the Redeemer, the new Eve united with
the new Adam. All her activity as a woman is of a
specifically different order. Mary worked alongside of
Jesus, not as an equal or as one engaged in the same
order of operation. Her office was additional and complementary to that of Christ, wholly subordinated to
it, and wholly that of a mother. In her own way, however, Mary also was totally dedicated to the service
of all her children. For them she offered her expiation, her merit and her intercession, all of which were
of immeasurable value as coming from the Coredemptress of the world.

In order to save her spiritual children from their
offenses and the consequences of their sins, Mary
gave her all; to her own universal role in the work of
salvation she dedicated her divine motherhood together with all its privileges, her incomparable fullness of grace, her boundless merit, and all the power
of expiation and intercession that resides in a mother's
heart. Furthermore, her public and official role in the
mystical body gave her a special right to be heard, not
in strict justice, but through divine benevolence, and
even through a sort of equity on God's part.

It is an accepted principle that the more pure a
person, the more power he has to make atonement.
The efficacy of Mary's expiation is based on this
principle. Hence it is clear that in this respect, as in
others, Mary is unexcelled among creatures, since her

work of expiation was enhanced by the privilege of the Immaculate Conception. Because of this privilege her union with God was so great that even the smallest offense against Him affected her deeply and caused her the most acute sorrow. Like her Son, but in her own way, she too had to expiate in her virginal and maternal heart all the sins of mankind, all its depravities, its crimes, its acts of vileness and impurity, its transgressions of every conceivable sort. She, too, saw all the moral failures of mankind, from the Fall to the revolt of Antichrist; saw mankind committing, as if driven by frenzy, sin after sin. The Immaculate foresaw them all, atoned for all.

The fullness of grace possessed by the Virgin most faithful and the purity of her acts of love were so pleasing in the sight of the three divine Persons of the Blessed Trinity that one might say They deigned to overlook the ingratitude of men, all the more so because her fullness of grace manifested itself in a maternal solicitude for each of us and gave her the power to atone in behalf of all her sinful children. Like a heroic mother, Mary offered herself to divine justice in order to make amends for the transgressions of her children. So often—is it not true?—a mother's Calvary comes from taking upon herself, out of love and mercy, the sins of her children in order to spare them the consequences of their folly.

It should be noted that, above all, it was her position as the Mother of God that made her feel most keenly not only the entire burden of mankind's ingratitude but even the smallest offense against a God who is so good. Every offense and every rebellious act against God produced the deepest sorrow in the heart of the Mother of God and of men, of the Mediatress between God and her children. Mary's unique position as the Mother of God gave her every action, great and small, an expiatory value that is incomparably superior to the value of all the penances and sufferings of the Church militant throughout all the centuries. To put it another way, the joy that even the smallest action of Mary gave to the Blessed Trinity was greater than the displeasure resulting from all the sins of mankind.

At the foot of the Cross Mary, in a supreme act of love for us, offered to God the Father His only Son in behalf of her other children, uniting her own merits as mother of the Redeemer with the infinite merits of Christ's Passion. Through this coredemptive atonement she obtained, in a manner that was subordinate but complementary to Christ's, the pardon of all the sins of mankind and the remission of the punishments due to all sins from the beginning to the end of the world. Her sacrifice as mother in union with that of Christ expiated all, erased all. That is why there is no sinner, even though he may have committed the most heinous crimes, who cannot put his absolute trust in the all-powerful and most merciful intercession of Mary. In fact, the Church herself invokes her as the advocate in hopeless situations and as the refuge of sinners.

3   A MOTHER'S MERITS

If men were to enjoy beatitude it was not enough to avert the chastisement due their sins. The Redeemer, in other words, had also to merit heaven for us. Atonement bears on guilt, and satisfaction on punishment, but merit on a positive good. Merit gives the right to eternal recompense, to the joys of paradise.

Christ alone could merit this divine happiness for us. As a matter of fact, His entire activity as the only-begotten Son of the Father became the means of gaining for us the grace of adoption, which is the seed of eternal glory for the true children of God, for those who are called to live in Him, being perfected in the unity of the Trinity. The somber background of sin which caused such unremitting sorrow in the heart of our Saviour was thus relieved by the thought of the great happiness in store for His redeemed. It was in this spirit that He prayed: "Father, I will that where I am, they also whom thou hast given me may be with me, in order that they may behold my glory." [4]

Christ wrought our salvation as head of the mystical body. He acted in our name and gained heaven for us. He merited for each of us all the graces and helps we need to achieve the highest levels of holiness. In the blood of Jesus there always has been, in every age of the history of the Church, and there always will be, even in the time of Antichrist, a divine and sanctifying power that is able to raise souls up to God and to convert the greatest sinners into the greatest saints. The Passion of Christ, in other words, is an inexhaustible source of holiness.

In her own way the Mother of God and of men, in union with her Son the Redeemer, also obtained for her children the power to become godlike through grace. She, too, wanted us to be conformed to her Son, the only-begotten Son of the Father, to be holy with His holiness, to share eternally with Him the same glory and the same splendors. Never forget that

[4] John 17:24.

Mary was and is a mother, and that it is in the nature of a mother not only to avert every evil from her children but above all to procure their true happiness.

Enlightened by her unexampled faith, Mary foresaw the marvels of grace and glory that awaited her children, both of the present and the future, if they were faithful to God. With all her heart she besought God to help her accomplish the great task of motherhood in behalf of her children. As the Immaculate, she had already accumulated, even before the Cross and even before becoming a mother, an immense store of spiritual treasures that were to serve the mystical body of Christ and all mankind. Through the merits of her prayer and her life she had already brought about the coming of the Messias into the world. But now that through her fiat at the Incarnation all humanity was officially in her care, she lived only for the salvation of all her children, dedicating her every act to the service of the total Christ in the mystical body. She realized infinitely better than we the indissoluble unity and solidarity of this body, with the result that her maternal love for the multitude of His brethren was only an extension of the love she had for Jesus Himself.

Mary's dignity as the Mother of God and her fullness of grace were productive of the greatest spiritual fruit for us. Each of her actions had a universal import; on each hung the destiny of mankind. Jesus alone excepted, no person was more closely associated with our eternal destiny and our most intimate graces than Mary our Mother, more mother than our mothers in the flesh, having given us, not the transitory life conceived in sin, but the life that is divine and eternal. Every mother brings forth life, but this mother has given us, in the order of grace, the very life of God.

It is difficult for us, if not impossible, to understand how great was the maternal concern that the Mother of God manifested for each of us, not only in the remarkable actions of her life but also in the most ordinary ones. In this respect we are almost like small children who cannot possibly realize how utterly their mother lives only for them. From the moment of her fiat at the Incarnation Mary, following her Son, lived only for us. God joined Mother and Son as partners in the same work of our salvation. Both the one and the other, each in his own way, merited heaven for us as well as all the graces needed to bring us there. They merited the grace of baptism and the grace of all the other sacraments, the grace to remain pure or to regain lost purity, the grace of conversion and spiritual progress, the grace of union, the grace of the inspirations that have raised us upward to God, the grace of the priesthood or, as the case may be, of the religious life—in short, all the different graces whereby each of our lives and that of the Church as a whole are advanced on the road that leads to the eternal splendors of the City of God.

In Mary herself, moreover, all the saints have their model. Through the grace that is hers as mother she is able to form each of her children according to the image of her only Son. For this reason there are no hopes that may not be fervently entertained by those who entrust themselves to Mary's guiding care.

4 A MOTHER'S SACRIFICE

Concern for the Father's glory dominated everything in the soul of Christ, even His fervent desire to accomplish our redemption. For, if the salvation of the world was a determining motive of His incarnation, in the mind of God and in the soul of Christ the ultimate reason could only be to secure God's glory. These two points of view, moreover, are not incompatible, but rather they complement each other in a marvelous way—which is to say that our redemption redounded to God's glory.

Thus, at the very moment of His coming into the world Christ prophetically offered Himself for us, revealing the love that was to bring about the Father's glory as well as our redemption. His "Behold, I come" indicated clearly what was the deepest sentiment in His soul; it showed that the basic orientation of the Son of God was always toward His Father. And when the moment of His Passion came, it was again His resolve to glorify the Father that determined the time for His leaving the world, so that, as He said, "the world may know that I love the Father, and that I do as the Father has commanded me. Arise, let us go from here." [5] In the mind of Christ the redemption of the world was precisely the highest glorification of God. Jesus fulfilled this sublime mission of His both as priest and victim.

Accordingly, the Christ of Golgotha is, first of all, a Christ-Priest offering to God the one sacrifice for the sins of mankind. His role and activity as priest shaped the course of all the concrete circumstances

[5] John 14:31.

surrounding the mystery of the Cross. It was as sovereign priest, and in a strictly priestly manner, that He accomplished His redemptive work. Everything He did had a specifically priestly character; everything had its source in His sacrificial oblation on the Cross, whether it be His atonement, His merit, His prayer, His power to sanctify souls—all came from the Cross.

Furthermore, His redemptive sacrifice marked the inauguration of a new, a Christian cult. If we want to know what were the inmost thoughts and feelings of the crucified Christ on Golgotha, it is only by seeking to penetrate the priestly character of His soul that we can discover them. Priest and victim at the same time, having both human and divine nature, by one and the same act He not only atoned for our sins and accomplished our redemption, but also offered to God such adoration, such thanksgiving, and such supplication as to render infinite glorification to the three divine Persons. Indeed, the praise and glory which Christ offered to God on Calvary is beyond measure; and to the end of time the Church in exercising her cult toward God will, in truth, have no other function than to perpetuate substantially the infinite effects of this redemptive sacrifice. It is not too much to say that the entire history of worship in the world converges upon, and finds its ultimate expression in this unique act of the priestly soul of Christ, the Mediator between men and God.

As everywhere in the life of Christ, Mary had her role on Golgotha. Standing at the foot of the Cross she united her sacrifice as mother with the sacrifice of the eternal Priest. Her oblation, it is true, was not that of a priest, but it was the highest sacrifice that the heart of a woman and mother can make: the offering up of her own Son. All her rights and privileges as mother she offered up unto God's glory. She understood as only she could that the voluntary self-immolation of the Word Incarnate gave to God the only praise and glory worthy of His grandeur and majesty. Rising above her own great sorrow, the worshipful Virgin, Mother of the eternal Priest, merged her soul with the soul of her Son and united herself with the acts of adoration, prayer and thanksgiving He offered to God. At this moment her soul enjoyed even more divine enlightenment than in the first days of the Incarnation. Thus united with Christ, she adored, she gave thanks, she offered supplication, she atoned.

The Church, needless to say, has always been deeply conscious of the unique role of the Mother of Jesus at the foot of the Cross. That is why she never celebrates the memorial of Christ's Passion without invoking Mary. In the Eucharistic sacrifice she commemorates, "in the first place," [6] the glorious Virgin Mary, who stood at the foot of the Cross and united her own sacrifice as mother with the oblation made by the priestly soul of her Son.

5 A MOTHER'S RANSOM

Accustomed as we are through the established teachings of our faith to live and think in terms of a world that has been redeemed, we do not always appreciate the full measure of the deliverance that Christ's coming brought to the souls of men. Without Him, we should still be slaves of sin, of hell, of Satan. By

[6] Canon of the Mass: "communicantes . . . in primis . . ."

one stroke, He freed us from them all. We know this,
our faith teaches it, but do we really appreciate its
full meaning? Perhaps those who know from experience what it means to have the burden of an enemy
occupation on one's back in time of war, perhaps
such, I say, are in a better position to understand
what a great boon it is to enjoy this inner freedom
and to be able to love God as His adopted children,
instead of being slaves of the devil. Christ our head
has gained for us the sovereign freedom of the children of God, so that we may now live, not in the
remorse of sin and in terror of chastisement, but in
the possession of a soul delivered from evil and cring-
ing fear. We can now look to God with filial hearts
and, like His Son, live in fellowship with the Father.
Every member of His mystical body shares with the
Saviour the joyful freedom of being a son of God, with
the heartfelt love and yearnings of a son.

In the deliverance of souls Mary again had a great
part. It was Christ alone who paid the price of our
redemption by freely giving His own life as the Word
Incarnate, but it was His Mother, remember, who
gave Him the blood of redemption. Together, with
one accord, they gave their consent to one and the
same sacrifice, offered by Jesus in His own Person,
by Mary in her maternal heart. If God had asked it,
Mary was prepared to immolate her Son herself, so
great was her desire to secure God's glory through expiation for sin and the redemption of souls. Together
with Jesus she expiated all, merited all, ransomed all,
saved all.

6   THE COREDEMPTRESS OF THE WORLD

From what has been said in this chapter we can see what a most extraordinary role the Mother of Christ had in the economy of our redemption. Associated with Christ the Redeemer in the entire work of our salvation, with Him she labored and strove to destroy evil in the world and restore all men to friendship with God. For all her children she has regained paradise. It is true, of course, that as spiritual head of the human race which was saved by His sacrifice on the Cross, Christ alone is the Redeemer. As priest and victim in one, He is the only Mediator between God and men. Everything pertaining to Him, we have said, had a sacrificial and priestly character, whether it be His atonement, His merits, or His acts of adoration, of praise and of supplication. In Mary, on the other hand, everything was a mother's, be it her coredemptive sufferings, her great merit, her all-powerful intercession, or her sacrificial act at the foot of the Cross.

As we have seen, the Word Incarnate gained our redemption in strict justice. By reason of His divine Person, all of His theandric actions—that is, His actions as the God-man—even the least of them, had an infinite value. Mary secured our salvation, not on an equal footing with Christ, but as a mother who merited the salvation of her children by the principle of congruity or fittingness, that is, in virtue of the special predilection she enjoyed before God as the Mother of the Saviour.[7] Mary herself, like the other

[7] Well known is the traditional Marian axiom, repeated by Pope Pius X (*Ad diem illum*, Feb. 2, 1904): "What Christ

members of the mystical body, received from Christ all she had, both her personal redemption and her co-redemptive power. She is not only one of the redeemed, but the foremost among them. Her Immaculate Conception and her coredemptive power in no way imply that she was not herself redeemed. On the contrary, these unprecedented privileges are the very fruits of having been redeemed in a more profound and more sublime manner than the other members of the mystical body. Both of these precious jewels, that is, both the Immaculate Conception and her core-demptive power, she owed to her Son. Mary's role is totally dependent on Christ and her redemptive work is wholly subordinated to the action of her Son, but at the same time she was indissolubly united with Him in His entire work of redemption. Far from putting her outside the economy of redemption, from the point of view of mankind her role as Coredemptress is in fact the primary and the most wonderful effect of the redemption of Christ.

In order to fathom this mystery in all its profundity, we must try to penetrate without reserve God's eternal plan for the world. It was part of this plan that a man and a woman were joined in partnership by God to accomplish one and the same work of restoration, even as both man and woman had been the instruments of the same general ruin. In Christ human nature atoned for itself, so to speak. Mary, always at His side, contributed to the work of redemption as partner and mother, but in the manner

---

merited condignly . . . Mary merits congruently." Modern Mariology extends this merit by "congruence" or fittingness so as to include the satisfactory and coredemptive value of the Mother of Christ's saving activity in our behalf.

of a woman. In other words, Christ suffered in the flesh, Mary in her heart. A mother is more pained by the sufferings of her son than by her own sorrow. This is how Mary contributed to the redemption of the world. The Word Incarnate, priest and victim in one, offered to His Father the one redemptive sacrifice. Mary was united with Him as a mother who consented to the heroic and exalted death of her Son. In Christ all is priestly; in Mary all is motherly. Christ and His Mother are the two persons who accomplished together and inseparably, each in his own way, our salvation.

Mary's role at the foot of the Cross was unique among the women who were present. The others could only receive the benefits of Christ's redemption. Mary not only received the *application* of the graces acquired by Christ, as did the other holy women, but she also shared with Him in the act by which all the graces of salvation were *acquired*. And this is what makes her role unique, namely, the fact that her consent as mother affected the very act that accomplished our redemption. By consenting to concur in our redemption, she acquired the greatest merit, even though her role was secondary and her claim only one of congruence or fittingness. To repeat, what gave such great worth to the merit resulting from her consent, and gave it the power to have redemptive value, was precisely the fact that the consent affected the very act of redemption.

Christ, may we say again, also died for Mary. One might even say that He died for her most of all; but He did so to gain for her, in addition to the privilege of the Immaculate Conception, a yet more splendid title, indeed, a title incomparably more splendid, namely, that of Coredemptress of the world. The Word Incarnate, the Redeemer, offered His life first of all for the redemption of His Mother, to merit for her the grace to become, in her turn and in conjunction with Him, the Coredemptress of all the other redeemed. Not only was she not removed from the economy of redemption, but she occupies such a high place in it that everything else was, in one sense, dependent upon her own coredemptive action, which, itself, derived its efficacy from the blood of her Son.

Such is the true character and perspective of the redemption of the world, a perspective which the Church is today beginning to unfold in all its amplitude. These new perspectives set in high relief one of the most fundamental truths of Christianity, heretofore more or less left in the shadows, namely, the truth of Mary's active and universal role in the work of salvation. In the centuries to come, it is safe to say, this prerogative of Mary will shine forth as one of the most beautiful jewels in her crown, second only to the incomparable grandeur of her divine motherhood. And in heaven all the elect will salute Christ as the only Saviour of men, and Mary as the one who was associated with Him as the Coredemptress of the world.[8]

[8] See Theological Note IX, p. 145.

six

She Who Keeps Watch Over the Church

"Suppliant Omnipotence."

On the night of Golgotha the faith of the Church was kept alive in the soul of Mary. Surrounded by the holy women, she received into her arms the excruciated body of her Son. At this moment all seemed hopelessly lost. Yet never in her entire history has the Church offered to God a more fervent act of inflexible hope than she did at this point, through Mary. The Mother of God knew that the Redemption had been accomplished. She awaited the future, serene and confident, her soul in perfect peace.

On Easter morning Christ rose from the tomb. The first appearance of the risen Saviour can only have been to His Mother. Human speech will ever be powerless to describe the meeting between Mary and her risen Son. The Gospels are silent on this point, and we will be wise to follow their example. But there can be no doubt that Jesus went first to see His Mother. The joy that she then experienced made her forget forever the Calvary that she had endured as a mother.

This first meeting was not the only one. Mary also saw Jesus in the forty days that followed the Resurrection, saw Him as victorious over death, radiant and glorious, saw and heard Him speak to His disciples of the kingdom of God, now at hand. Still preoccupied with thoughts of earthly greatness, the disciples asked the risen Saviour, "Lord, wilt thou at this time restore the kingdom to Israel?" Jesus took advantage of the occasion to raise their minds to spiritual horizons, transcending the material world. "It is not for you," He admonished them, "to know the times or dates which the Father has fixed by his own authority; but you shall receive power when the Holy Spirit comes upon you, and you shall be witnesses for me in Jerusalem and in all Judea and Samaria and even to the very ends of the earth." [1]

Then, after He had said this, He was lifted up to heaven before their eyes. As He ascended, His last act over them was one of benediction. In a few moments a cloud took Him out of their sight. Still gazing heavenward, watching Jesus as He disappeared, they saw standing by them two men in white garments, who said: "Men of Galilee, why do you stand looking up to heaven? This Jesus who has been taken up from you into heaven, will come in the same way as you have seen him going up to heaven." [2]

After that, they returned to Jerusalem and went up to the Cenacle, their hearts filled with great joy. Gathered there were Peter and John, James and Andrew, Philip and Thomas, and the other disciples of the Lord. All with one mind "continued steadfastly

[1] See Acts 1:6-8.
[2] Acts 1:9-11.

in prayer with the women and Mary, the mother of Jesus . . ." [3]

I   NURTURING THE INFANT CHURCH

Instinctively, after the departure of their Lord and Master, the Apostles and disciples gathered around Mary. She, the Mother of Jesus, abided among them, watching over the infant Church with the tenderness of a mother. Through her mediatory and all-powerful prayer she besought her Son to send down the Spirit of God, who would change the hearts of men and the face of the earth. And when at Pentecost the Spirit of her Son descended on the Apostles, Mary was present. And like her Son after the Resurrection, the Holy Spirit, before diffusing Himself in the souls of the disciples, came first to Mary, bringing her His fullness in unparalleled measure. This presence of Mary amid the infant Church is most significant and revealing. It is always thus; it is always through her that the Holy Spirit comes to the souls of men.

It was her being the Mother of Jesus that moved the Apostles to esteem and venerate Mary. To her they brought their doubts and queries, and like a most loving mother, she reassured them in their anxieties and answered their questions, many of which bore on matters that only she knew. She had been the privileged witness of the life of Jesus, of His divine sonship, of His virginal conception and miraculous birth, of His childhood, and of His life of inmost union with the Father. She enlightened the Apostles and Evangelists on all these things that she kept ever in her heart.

[3] Acts 1:14.

Furthermore, as one of the circle of first Christians, the Mother of Jesus took part with them in the Eucharistic sacrifice, participating in the breaking of bread and communicating in the body and blood of her Son. If the primitive Church manifested such ardent fervor in the service of Christ, one of the chief sources of it, we can be sure, was the presence of Mary and her all-powerful intercession. Never, in offering the Eucharistic sacrifice, has the Church militant experienced such fervent adoration and supplication as she did in the primitive Church, when those who had been present with Mary on Golgotha again gathered with the Mother of Jesus to offer the same sacrifice in common prayer and adoration. And when the Apostles went forth from the sacrifice to labor and struggle for the kingdom of Christ, Mary accompanied them in prayer. Her solicitous surveillance followed them everywhere as they went out to gain the first successes of the primitive Church among the Gentiles.

More and more, however, Mary's soul began to live in the atmosphere of the world beyond, being irresistibly drawn toward her Son. The Mother of God was approaching the evening of life. Through her great faith, which produced the deepest understanding and peace in her soul, she already enjoyed the highest supernatural insights short of the beatific vision, giving her a living awareness of the divine presence in all things round about her. So exalted now was the mystic transport of her soul that without a constant special grace from God she could not have endured to remain united with her mortal body.

The Church benefited to the fullest degree from this immeasurable spiritual fruitfulness of the Mother of the Word Incarnate, elevated as she now was to the highest possible summits of the transforming union that a creature can enjoy and yet remain in this life. The ardent love burning in her heart helped to sustain the Church of Jesus in her daily struggles. In fact, the treasury of merits gained by the Mother of Christ was so great that the Church militant will be able to draw from it during all the long centuries of her existence without ever depleting it.

At last, Mary's life on earth was ended. The day came when, in a supreme outpouring of love, the Mother of God rejoined her Son forever. Now they were "perfected in unity." [4] Her Son, eternal Wisdom and Thought now one with her, bestowed upon His Mother a beatitude rich beyond measure and enduring without end. Soon thereafter, her virginal body, incorrupt, was reunited with her soul in heaven, where it shares in the glory of the risen body of her Son. And the angels and saints, full of wonder and admiration, could behold reflected in the countenance of His Mother the features and lineaments of Jesus.

2   "SUPPLIANT OMNIPOTENCE"

As on earth, so in eternity the activity of the Mother of Christ follows the same pattern as that of her Son. For both, the time for meriting and expiating is past. Yet Jesus is always at the right hand of the Father now, more the Saviour than ever. Though the work of redemption is over, the application of its benefits to the individual members of the mystical body continues. This work of application represents the second phase of our salvation, and in this phase the Mother

[4] John 17:23.

and the Son remain, as always, indissolubly united. It is, in fact, most fitting and equitable that they who together acquired the infinite treasure of the merits of our redemption, should continue together in distributing its fruits to all the redeemed. For the truth is that the acquisition and the distribution of all graces constitute two correlative and complementary phases of the same work of reconciling the world with God.

What needs to be stressed here is that the universal mediation of Mary is not confined to the mere distribution of all graces. To regard it as such would be an unwarranted minimization of its full tenor and import. One cannot give what one does not have. If Mary's intervention plays a part in the application of all the benefits acquired by the Saviour, it is because on Calvary she was associated with Christ in the very act of our redemption. These two successive and complementary phases of our salvation, that is, the phase of acquisition and the phase of distribution of all graces, go together and are inseparable and irrevocable. What this means is simply that in heaven Mary is the Distributress of all graces because at the foot of the Cross she was the Coredemptress of the world.

Furthermore, if in the life of Christ on earth prayer and adoration seemed to play a secondary role as compared with His great redemptive suffering, such is not the case now. In the second phase of the economy of salvation, prayer and supplication constitute the major role. In other words, all the graces acquired on Golgotha are applied to individual souls only through the mediatory intercession of Jesus. For this reason St. Paul represents Christ as always living to make intercession for us.[5] This concise phrase of St. Paul expresses the whole sum and substance of Christ's activity in eternity in behalf of His Church. In His life in eternity He is ever mindful of us. He never, so to speak, takes His eyes off us, not even for a moment. In the beatific vision He sees clearly what the Church's needs are, and from His heart unceasing supplication goes forth to the Father. God alone, it is true, has the power to make our lives divine by grace, but the Blessed Trinity does not dispense grace to souls except through the prayer and supplication of Jesus. As head of the Church, He prays for all the material and spiritual helps she requires to perform her mission on earth and to bring about among mankind the triumph of God's cause and justice.

Here again, in His intercessory role, we find Mary associated with Christ. United with her Son in His supplication, she too is always before the Father's countenance and never ceases to intercede for each one of us. All nations as well as all individuals are regarded as her children. Her maternal love embraces all in one and the same prayer. Indeed, how could a mother see her children in distress and fail to make ardent supplication to God in their behalf? Mary knows from experience that her intercession is all-powerful. She has only to turn to her Son to obtain from the Father, through her Son, any and every grace, it matters not which, of salvation and holiness. When she intercedes, God grants all. The Son cannot refuse His Mother anything. She, on the other hand, asks only what will promote the eternal happiness of her children and the greater glory of the Father.

[5] See Hebrews 7:25.

In her intercession Mary, it need hardly be said, relies in the first place on the infinite merits that her Son acquired on the Cross. Beyond that, however, her own role as Coredemptress, and her own great merit, also give her the right to be heard. Hence, there is not a single grace that the unfailingly efficacious prayer of the Mother of God cannot obtain. The Church knows this, none better, and she never tires of repeating over and over: "Pray for us sinners." In every peril, in every need, she turns to the Mother of Jesus, having experienced a thousand times and more the sovereign intercessory power of Mary. Quite properly, therefore, does the Church give her the striking title of "Suppliant Omnipotence," [6] that is, she to whom God always hearkens.

3　THE "AQUEDUCT" OF ALL GRACES

Mary's role in heaven is not confined to prayer; it also embodies action, action that is wholly maternal in character. It is difficult to determine with precision the nature of this action except to say that we cannot escape attributing to it a maximum degree of reality, so long as we are careful to distinguish its operation from the manner in which Christ and His ministers act upon souls.

Christ acts in His Church as priest and king. Through the offering of the holy sacrifice of the Mass, of which He is the principal priest, and through the sanctification of souls, Christ exercises His eternal priesthood in a manner that always makes it present and efficacious. Through His visible representatives, authorized by Him, the Word Incarnate

[6] "Omnipotentia supplex."

Himself continues to offer the sacrifice of His Church and to administer the sacraments. It is Christ Himself who baptizes, gives absolution, ordains His priests, joins His faithful in marriage, and who at the end of their life prepares them through extreme unction to pass from this life to His Father's house in heaven.

Christ's priestly action sanctifies souls; it does so in the capacity of an instrument of the Blessed Trinity, that is, insofar as His action as Christ is the action of the Person of the Word. For this reason the sanctifying action of Jesus reaches to the inmost being of the soul, imparting grace and all the infused virtues. He is the special, the privileged instrument through whom all the movements and inspirations of the Holy Spirit are communicated, from the initial stirrings of grace preparatory to conversion to the divinely inspired movements of the souls of the men and women who have attained the highest stages of the transforming union. Through Christ the Mediator are transmitted whatever graces God bestows. The priests of the Church are only His humble instruments, entirely dependent upon Him, the visible representatives and simple intermediaries of the action by which the Blessed Trinity, through the humanity of Christ, imparts to men the sanctifying life of grace.

However, in the communicating of grace as everywhere else, Mary and Jesus work together. And here, as always, it is in her capacity as mother that she is associated with this action of her Son that reaches to the inmost being of the soul. The question is whether Mary's maternal office in this respect is limited to the power of her prayer or whether it goes beyond her intercessory office. Strictly speaking, her activity as our Mediatress, with its truly universal and all-embracing efficacy, would be enough to merit her the title of Distributress of all graces to a unique degree, incomparably more so than is true of all the saints combined. For her mediation is of a different order than that of the saints; it is that of the Coredemptress of the world, the associate of the one Saviour of men in the very act by which we were redeemed.

Nevertheless, if, as is true, Mary was and is unceasingly united with Christ in all phases of His mediatory action, why not also with that part of His action which has to do specifically with the communication of grace? Doubtless, her role in this respect is not priestly or sacramental, but one in keeping with her office as mother, no more and no less. Every mother, it should be noted, brings forth life. From this point of view Mary was not an exception. In fact, God in His eternal plan bestowed on her the office of a twofold motherhood. By her divine motherhood she brought forth a God in the flesh; by her spiritual motherhood she gives birth every day to the life of God in the souls of men. There is no reason why we should not attribute to her spiritual motherhood all possible objective reality and acknowledge her as a real instrument in the supernatural action by which we receive the divine life of grace.

At the foot of the Cross Mary gave us spiritual birth, having conceived us spiritually by her fiat at the Incarnation. Now, in heaven, she puts forth every effort, in a manner of speaking, to lift us up to God and to form Christ in every one of us. This Mother of men in the order of divine grace seeks to promote only what is eternal and divine. It is not the ephemeral life of earth that she imparts, but the life that is eternal. Needless to say, it is not she who baptizes, confirms, and administers the sacraments. Nevertheless, it is she who brings us the life of the Blessed Trinity. For, to repeat, Mary like every mother is a giver of life. She works with her Son in bringing sanctifying grace to all the children of God: He as the head of the mystical body and as priest and mediator; she as mother, all-powerful in action, unceasingly moved and guided by the three divine Persons of the Blessed Trinity. God the Father chose her as the Mother of all His adopted children; the Son Incarnate made her a partner in His entire work of redemption; and in the sanctification of souls the Holy Spirit employs her as an instrument of predilection. Accordingly, we can say in all truth that nothing comes about in the supernatural order without the mediatory action of Mary.

4 "MORE MOTHER THAN QUEEN"

Mary, as we have seen, is associated with Christ and the Blessed Trinity in the acquisition and distribution of all graces. But Mary plays a part in yet another aspect of the Trinitarian life, namely, in the governance of the world. The Blessed Trinity governs the world, but not without Mary. At first, we may find this thought surprising, but it is nonetheless true. It is a truth that follows from the fact that Mary is associated with Christ in all of His activity.

In considering the activity of Christ, we must include His governing of the world. There can be no question that the government and direction of the world falls within the scope of Christ's jurisdiction. For Christ is king, and His kingship embraces the whole universe. He possesses the fullness of kingly power, and through Him the world is being directed to its ultimate destiny. The angels themselves are only the humble servants of Christ the King. He orders and commands as Lord of all the universe. There is nothing that escapes His sovereign rule. Not even the smallest atom stirs without His permission or concurrence. The entire spirit world, including man's spirit, as well as the whole physical universe, is ordained to serve His glory. God has made all creation subject to His sovereign power. Like a ruler who governs and directs His people to their goal, the Word Incarnate directs all intellect toward truth and all will toward happiness and beatitude.

But Christ the King has made His Mother His associate in governing the world. In union with Him she illuminates the world of pure spirits, and all the angels respond to her slightest wish. Mankind, too, and the whole Church are under Mary's guiding, motherly care. Of course, her rule is not the same as Christ's. She is not a Christ-King of the feminine sex. As mentioned in an earlier chapter, to regard her as such would be a gross misconception. In the realm of kingship as elsewhere, Mary maintains her role as woman, as companion of Christ, and as the Mother of men. Mary's sovereign rule is one that is proper to her, a rule that is characteristic of a woman and a mother. It is nevertheless a supremely real and efficacious rule; and since her merit, her atonement, her prayer, and her mediatory action extend to the entire mystical body, it is a rule that is not less universal for being that of a woman and mother.

There are things that we feel more than we know how to express. This is perhaps true regarding

Mary's role in Christ's kingship. The Church seems to take for granted the fact of Mary's rule over men and the universe. On every possible occasion she exalts Mary as queen: "Queen of angels and men, Queen of virgins and confessors, Queen of martyrs and all saints, Queen not only for her excellence and by reason of the primacy of honor that she enjoys, but Queen in the exercise of real dominion and sovereign rule; Queen, that is, of the world, Queen of heaven and earth, Queen of the universe."

Mary, then, is queen, but queen in the way of a mother, serving all her children, guiding them in their most personal and intimate life, not so much by law and precept as by kindly prompting and persuasion, with an affectionate smile on her countenance as she goes about bestowing a mother's tender care on all her children, on the lowliest no less than on the more fortunate. In fact, the more humble and lowly her children, the more mother she is to them. And the more we put ourselves in Mary's guiding care, the more quickly she leads us up to God.

In union with Christ, Mary guides the entire Church militant on the road to the City of God. But Mary's rule is marked, above all, by the supreme grace of her motherhood. She rules and directs souls with the power of a mother's smile and the irresistible attraction of a mother's sweetness. With a mother's intuition she is ever alert, one might say, to yield to the supremely sovereign and kingly action of her Son, keeping herself in the background, for even in her own sovereign rule over the universe Mary is "more mother than queen." [7]

[7] St. Thérèse of the Child Jesus, *Novissima verba*, Aug. 23, 1897.

seven

God's Masterpiece

> *God could have created a more magnificent universe, but He could not have created anything more beautiful than His Mother.*

Through faith we learn that Mary is immaculate, a woman endowed with divine motherhood. We learn that she is the Queen of angels and the Mother of men; that by reason of her sublime mission on earth and in heaven, she occupies a unique place among God's works and creatures. This mission, moreover, was wholly ordained to our salvation, and in accomplishing it she worked as the inseparable partner of the Word Incarnate in His mission. She is at the summit of creation, close by her Son. Mary is, in truth, God's masterpiece, second only to Jesus.

I THE PRIMACY OF CHRIST

In extolling the grandeurs of Mary we must not overlook the fact that in all things the primacy belongs to Christ. The Word Incarnate is the supreme masterpiece of the Blessed Trinity, which is the Alpha and Omega of all that is. Equal to His Father by His divine nature, the Word Incarnate is at the same time a man like us. He is, so to speak, the synthesis of the whole universe, incorporating by His twofold nature all the riches of both God and creation.

From the first moment of His coming into the world, the Word Incarnate stood as the crown of all the works of God, inasmuch as the hypostatic order of Christ comprises every order of being, namely, the order of nature, of grace, and of glory. It takes only a moment's reflection on this wonder of a God present in person among men to realize that it is without parallel, and that not a single being, from the smallest atom to the most exalted angel, can withdraw from the ultimate destiny of being ordained to the glory of the Word Incarnate. Before this sovereign primacy of Christ, which is as striking as it is evident, we can but stand in awe and admiration.

In the present order of divine providence, everything has been made subject to the universal causality of Christ, for Christ's causality is truly universal. By the free determination of the Father, who is the primordial source of all good, Christ is the all-inclusive cause of our salvation: the expiatory, satisfactory, meritorious, impetratory, efficient, exemplary, and final cause. All redemption and salvation of sinful man, all movement of the universe, all adoration and praise offered up by the angels and archangels and the blessed in heaven—all this comes to pass through the priestly mediation of the Word Incarnate, "through whom the angels pour forth their praises." [1] Thus, on every level of being and operation Christ's unique mediation stands out in bold relief. Christ Jesus is the sole Mediator between God and man. In

[1] "Per quem laudant angeli" (various Prefaces).

the words which conclude the Canon of the Mass, "through Him, and with Him, and in Him is . . . all honor and glory." [2]

2 OUR PREDESTINATION IN MARY

After twenty centuries of Christianity we are accustomed to attributing absolute primacy and headship to Christ, the only Mediator and Saviour of the world, Priest and King of the universe. As we have seen, however, in our own day the Church has begun to take more notice than formerly of a complementary truth, a truth that had been left—providentially, it would seem—in the background and shadows. We are beginning more and more to understand the exceptional role which a privileged creature had in God's plan, a role, however, which is totally dependent on Christ's role and is ordained to His glory, and which in no way detracts from the sovereign dominion that the Word Incarnate exercises over all of God's works. More than heretofore we are discovering Mary as the Coredemptress of the world.

Being the Mother of a Saviour-God, Mary is associated with Him as the Mother of His entire mystical body as well. She is the universal Mediatress, with a place next to the only Mediator. Through Him, with Him, in Him, and on behalf of Him, Mary also is a universal cause of our salvation—expiatory, satisfactory, meritorious, and impetratory, perhaps efficient cause, certainly exemplary and final cause. It may seem bold to say that we have been predestined in Mary as well as in Christ, but it is true and we need

[2] "Per ipsum et cum ipso et in ipso . . . omnis honor et gloria" (end of Canon).

not hesitate to say it. She who is both the Mother of Christ and our Mother, has a hand in our own pre-destination, not only in its initial phase but also in its ultimate conclusion.[3] As always, however, her role here is totally dependent on the Word Incarnate and Redeemer, yet its extension through the economy of salvation is not less universal than His.

Most assuredly, all that we have we owe to Christ —but we also owe it to His Mother. It has pleased God to pardon our transgressions and to deliver us from the eternal and temporal punishment due to our sins, only by taking into account the coredemptive atonement and sufferings of Mary. And God has decreed to bestow His grace on redeemed mankind only by taking cognizance of Mary's great merit as mother, as well as in view of the merits of His Son. God comes to our assistance only by her intercession. He has predestined us to be conformed to the image of both the Mother and the Son. From all eternity the all-powerful and most merciful Blessed Trinity has freely determined to pour forth grace into souls only through the hands of Mary. Furthermore, at the end of time, when the fullness of Christ's mystical body will have been consummated, the whole body will redound to Mary's glory, and she in turn will surrender all praise to Christ, and Christ to God. "For all things are yours . . . and you are Christ's, and Christ is God's." [4]

3   THE GLORY OF DIVINE MOTHERHOOD

The focal point of all the privileges and pre-emi-

[3] See Theological Note X, p. 148.
[4] I Corinthians 3:22-23.

nence of Mary, the center from which radiate all her other glories, is her divine motherhood. It is this which lies at the root and source of her whole life and character, this which brings her within the orbit of the hypostatic order to the very confines of divinity. This it is, also, that gives Mary the honor of having the same Son as God the Father; and not only does the Father find in Him His infinite pleasure, but Mary also is privileged to approach this same eternal Son with the warm and tender affection of a mother. Both the Father and Mary find in Him the ultimate reason of their whole life and being. The Son is all to His Father and all to His Mother. For both, His divine presence results in the possession of infinite beatitude.

No sooner had Mary become the Mother of God than she began to be aware of hitherto unexperienced relationships with each other of the three divine Persons of the Blessed Trinity. Having been elevated to the highest possible dignity that can be bestowed on a mere creature, the Mother of God could feel at home even in the supernatural domain of the three divine Persons. Handmaid of the Father, Mother of the Son, Spouse of the Holy Spirit, Mary was a partner in the entire plan of the world's redemption; and inasmuch as the influence of her action extended to the whole mystical body and to all of God's works, she was, by grace, "the complement of the Trinity." [5]

In addition to realizing that she was the Mother

[5] This traditional phrase must not be interpreted to mean that Mary shares in the essential nature of the Trinity and in the so-called *ad intra* operations of the three divine Persons, but that she is related to the Trinity in an accidental and complementary manner, as an instrument of the Trinity in the sanctification of souls.

of God, Mary also saw her divine motherhood grow into a spiritual motherhood embracing all mankind, for her Son was not only the Saviour but also the first-born of many brethren. From the moment of her fiat at the Incarnation Mary was dedicated heart and soul to the plan of salvation; she was committed to it in the concrete circumstances in which it was to be brought about, circumstances that had been conceived and decreed by God from all eternity. Accordingly, to the redemptive incarnation of the Son corresponds the coredemptive motherhood of Mary. This motherhood, both divine and spiritual, stands forth in the same clear light as the predestination of Christ Himself. In other words, the mystery of both Mother and Son is to be understood in the light of one and the same eternal decree by which mankind was ordained to receive the divine mercy. Hence, as the Mother of the Saviour-God, Mary became His closest confidante, His loyal and devoted companion, accomplishing with Him the same work of salvation.

In view of what we have just said, it is not surprising that throughout Sacred Scripture and the history of mankind as recorded there, even as in the eternal thought of God, the Mother and the Son always appear together, marching toward the fulfillment of a common destiny. In short, though the aspects of the mystery of salvation represented by Mary and Jesus are different, they are complementary, so that fundamentally the mystery of Jesus and that of Mary constitute but one mystery of salvation. The activity of both transcends time and space. Together, in their every action, they held the destiny of the world in their hands: Jesus as the Word Incarnate, the one Saviour, Priest and King; Mary as the Mother of

Jesus, exercising her motherly influence on each of us.

It would be idle to try to appraise such divine greatness in the light of mere reason. Only the light of God, which faith permits us to share, can give us this true perspective of mankind; only this light reveals mankind as journeying through history under the united action and direction of Mary and Jesus, both as saviour-workers, but each in his own way. In this perspective Christ, assuredly, stands at the center of the world, but God has also given Mary a share in ruling the universe. He has put the scepter of the world in her hands as well as in those of Christ.

4 FULLNESS OF GRACE

Mary's exalted mission made it imperative that she be endowed with the fullness of grace, knowledge, power and glory that she needed to perform her two-fold task of Mother and Mediatress: Mother of God and of men, Mediatress before the one Mediator, and, through Him, with Him and in Him, Mediatress before the Blessed Trinity.

In the first place, then, the Mother of the total Christ had to possess in the fullest measure all those riches of sanctifying grace which permit a simple creature to live in intimate fellowship with God. Accordingly, from the instant of her conception, the Blessed Trinity, which is the primordial source of the divine life of grace, lavished upon her such a fullness of holiness that the Immaculate surpasses in divine purity and grace all the angels and saints combined. Not only was Mary without sin, but her soul, made divine by grace, shone with the splendor of the

Father, was illuminated with the wisdom of the Word, and partook of the burning love of the Spirit of Love: all in all, the veritable masterpiece of nature and grace.

We need to reflect on this singular privilege of being alone immaculate and without sin among a race that is comprised wholly of sinful members; for only by reflecting on it shall we begin to have some faint idea of the profusion of grace and charismatic gifts with which Mary was endowed, and which attended her in ever greater measure as the mystery of her mission unfolded so that she might be made ready for her place in the hypostatic order, that is, in the mystery of a God in the flesh.

At the hour of the Incarnation the angel himself who brought the divine message could not but have marveled at this fullness of grace in a daughter of men. For Mary, it was the moment when the grace that was hers as virgin blossomed into the immeasurable fullness of grace that was hers as the Mother of God. From that moment, all her thoughts and desires as woman—indeed, as a woman become the Mother of the Word!—all her conscious life, in fact, received its impress from her most extraordinary union with the life of the Trinity; for into this Trinitarian life she was admitted, and in it she abided, in consequence of her intimate association with the Son. She lived with Him, and through Him she participated in the eternal communion between the Father and the Spirit of Love, to be henceforth associated with all the works of the Blessed Trinity. The wisdom of the Word enlightened her understanding and directed her entire life. Though yet living by faith, with its attendant shadows and obscurities, she was even now preserved from those failings of the human mind that are the common heritage of mankind, namely, from error, from ignorance as distinct from nescience,[6] and from aberrations of judgment in her understanding. Furthermore, in her heart she was never for a moment, or in the smallest measure, found deviating from the path of the most perfect righteousness. Her will was immovably fixed on Love Itself.

It is beyond our power to grasp the sublime transformation in God that was wrought in the soul of the Mother of the Word, a transformation that so penetrated to the inmost depths of her being as to determine the course and character of even her most commonplace actions. The least we can say—and we can say it with certainty—is that from the beginning she enjoyed such fullness of grace as to find herself immediately, not only in the transforming union, but in such a high degree of that union as no other creature on earth can ever attain, even after a long lifetime of spiritual growth and perfection. Consequently, all of her actions were performed under special impulse of the Holy Spirit, and for this reason they were invested with such great coredemptive merit and atonement as will never be equalled by all the combined works of the Church militant until the end of time.

The fact is that any comparison of Mary's fullness of grace with that of other saints fails to bring out sufficiently her superiority. A better term of compari-

[6] Mary was subject to nescience but not to ignorance. Nescience is absence of knowledge that is not expected or required or possible in a person, whereas ignorance is the lack of knowledge one could or should have. Nescience is a simple negation, ignorance a privation.—Translator's note.

son is Christ's grace of headship. Here, however, we must steadfastly insist on the infinite distance that separates Mary from her Son, true God in the flesh. Christ's human soul, like Mary's, was also endowed with sanctifying grace to such a degree that His every action as God-man was performed under constant impulse and prompting of the Holy Spirit. Through His fullness of grace, He was enabled to perform His theandric actions (that is, His actions as God-man living among men) with supreme and final perfection.

However, there is this difference, among others, between Christ's fullness of grace and Mary's, namely, that the holiness of Christ was whole and complete from the moment of His incarnation, as if by personal descent of God's holiness upon a man, whereas Mary's fullness of grace was susceptible of continuous and progressive increase through all of her actions. Unceasingly moved by the Holy Spirit in everything she did, the Mother of God and of men always responded unhesitatingly, never committing the slightest fault or imperfection. The decisive influence of the gifts of the Holy Spirit upon her soul, while all-pervasive from the beginning, advanced yet further with each successive action in her life. Thus she acquired progressively, in behalf of Christ's entire mystical body, a store of merit and satisfaction which the Church militant will never exhaust. And now, in the possession of glory and consummated holiness in heaven, she is of all creatures the one most like unto God.

5 FULLNESS OF KNOWLEDGE

The first condition under which Mary was privileged to share, heart and soul, in the knowledge of God's eternal plan for her and for the world was faith, the ardent faith that illuminates the soul. On earth she never saw God face to face. Like us, she had to walk humbly and obediently by the obscure light of faith alone, without having the higher sort of knowledge possessed by the angels and without experiencing, even intermittently, those charismatic privileges which belong to the beatific vision. As a matter of fact, we must carefully avoid every exaggeration of pen and speech that might suggest such a condition. The status of the humble Virgin Mary on earth was that of a wayfarer, still awaiting the vision of glory. In this respect she differed from Christ. For, as the Son of God, Christ unceasingly beheld the presence of His Father and possessed complete knowledge of God's entire eternal plan. Somewhat in the manner of the angels, He had a complete and exhaustive knowledge of the whole universe, down to the last detail. But all this He owed to the fact, unique and without parallel, that He was substantially united to the divine Person of the Word. Because of this union, even on earth His soul enjoyed the state of the blessed and the vision of glory, to which state and vision He came to lead the elect.

In considering Mary's fullness of knowledge, nothing is served by attributing to her such privileges and prerogatives as do not accord with the condition of the Mother of God still living by faith. True, hers was a faith enlightened by the gifts, the most illuminating and the most enrapturing gifts, of the Holy Spirit; yet the enlightenment of her faith could not approach the radiant vision of the light inaccessible in heaven. True, also, that through the intellectual charismatic gifts relating to prophecy, she received the many illuminations that she needed to fulfill her mission as universal Mediatress. But there is absolutely no reason for claiming for her any prerogatives that are incompatible with the order of faith.

In this, moreover, we are not left to our own thoughts and opinions. The gospel itself points the way. It shows Mary as being sometimes surprised and astonished, as sometimes puzzled and only dimly understanding certain things and events around her. These and similar experiences were, in fact, intended by Providence to increase her merit through faith. But even though she lived by faith, through her burning love and charity she could rise immeasurably above the limited comprehension accessible to faith, thus in a way loving more than knowing. Even in the sufferings laid upon her as Coredemptress, her soul was fixed fast on God through such complete surrender to Him as can be surpassed only in the beatific vision.

In Christ all this was different. Even on earth His soul lived in eternity, possessing at the very hour of His most bitter torments the steadfast peace of the vision of God. This continuous beholding of the Father's presence and of the whole drama of redemption, instead of lessening His suffering, only made Him realize all the more the selfishness of men and the malice of sin. Yet, as in the blessed, so in Him the eternally abiding splendors of the beatific vision overshadowed and dominated all. Mary, on the other hand, stands as the model of holiness in the order of faith. It was love, not the vision of glory, that animated and inspired her entire mission and mystery as Coredemptress. Love was the hidden source from which sprang and blossomed all her virtues.

Since the Assumption, however, we must accord to Mary a vision and knowledge of all those divine mysteries that her mission as Mediatress requires her to know in order to exercise her role in governing the world. In heaven she has a vision of all things in the illuminations from the Word and in the complementary illuminations that she receives from beholding the radiant countenance of the Father. Her vision and glory transcend those of all other creatures in heaven, so that the angels as well as men may look to her for enlightenment and understanding even in regard to the smallest details of the whole universe. As the Mother of God and of men, as the Queen of angels and of the world, she possesses a vision and knowledge that in all probability equals in extension, though not in depth and intensity, the knowledge of Christ Himself, that is to say, the so-called knowledge of vision of the three divine Persons of the Blessed Trinity. Mary, in short, sees and knows all. In the present order of divine providence nothing escapes the knowledge and vision of Mary.

6 FULLNESS OF POWER

On earth the power of Mary went unsuspected, hidden in the depths of her soul. Insofar as she exercised it at all, it was in the moral sphere of prayer and coredemptive atonement, seen only by God. As for the rest, the Mother of Christ worked no miracles, at least while her Son was still living in the world. Nevertheless, already on earth her spiritual activity in behalf of the Church extended to all men, to all ages and to all places, reaching even, by its indirect influence, all the angels and all beings of the universe.

But it was only after she had gone to heaven that she began to exercise the full scope of her power. Now that she has entered the abode of the elect, the Blessed Trinity performs no work without Mary. As was said earlier, God governs the world through Mary. She possesses all-powerful intercession and full freedom of action. As Distributress of all graces, she is always, every instant, interceding in our behalf. The destiny of all souls and of all nations is in her care and direction. Christ Himself, the supreme head of the Church, acts upon the souls of men only through Mary. He has made her the repository of all the blessings of His redemption. The Mother of God is ever at the right hand of her Son, sharing His glory, keeping watch over the salvation of the world. Indeed, the power she exercises is in a certain respect unlimited.[7]

Moreover, being an instrument of all God's works, she exercises dominion over the entire spirit world as well. In the present phase of the economy of salvation, therefore—and this is not exaggeration—not a single grace is imparted, not a single miracle wrought, without the intercession and mediatory action of Mary. Christ has entrusted all His powers to Mary, and God Himself exercises His omnipotent power in the world through the hands of Mary.

[7] "Permissa ei poene immensa potestate" (Leo XIII, Adjutricem populi, Sept. 5, 1895).

7 FULLNESS OF GLORY

For the Mother of God the tribulations of this life are past. Like Christ, however, she had to suffer before entering into glory. Sorrow was like an inseparable companion of her life. A true daughter of men, she shared with them all their miseries, sin excepted. Doubtless, God, who is a God of Love, could have spared His Mother all the sufferings and sorrows to which the sons of Adam are heir. He could have placed her in a state of innocence [8] and happiness hearkening back to the time before the Fall. But God in His wisdom deemed it better to allow her to experience not only suffering but also death, both of which are penalties that have been imposed on all human nature.

But there was a difference. In Mary the transitory afflictions which she suffered in this life were not for the purpose of expiating her personal sins, for she had none. In her, as in Christ, there was no trace of any moral fault; and if, as is the case, she accepted all her sufferings joyfully and heroically, it was to imitate Christ and to accomplish with Him the same common ends of redemption. Far from trying to avoid her task of expiation, she dedicated herself to it with her whole heart and soul. Let it be remembered, also, that her sensibilities were so acute and perceptive that even the least sorrow affected her most painfully. Sharing as she did in God's own

[8] Mary, of course, was innocent in the sense of being without sin; but she did not possess certain preternatural gifts, such as impassibility and immortality, with which Adam and Eve were endowed before the Fall. See Theological Note V, p. 137.—Translator's note.

light of understanding, Mary had a poignant awareness of the malice of sin in all its ramifications. Consequently, her life as Coredemptress, like that of
Jesus, was filled with unremitting sorrow. No other
human suffering even comes close to Mary's Calvary
and suffering as a mother. Beyond question, had she
not received special grace and assistance, the Mother
of Jesus should also have died of sorrow at the foot
of the Cross.

When, at last, the end of her time on earth had
come, Mary accepted death as willingly as she had
accepted suffering. As always, so now she lovingly
embraced God's will, counting her death as one last
testimony of her perfect conformity with her Son,
with whom she was always united for the redemption of the world and the glorification of the Father.
It was neither old age nor sickness that brought on
her death; it was simply a final transport of love, the
most beautiful and most sublime outpouring of love
that had come from a human heart since the day
when the crucified Christ poured forth His love from
the heart of a God.

Mary's death was more like a sleep, a dormition, to
use the word of the liturgy. Not that she only seemed
to be dead—far from it, for Mary died as surely as
we shall die, and there was a brief interval when her
virginal body was changed into a lifeless, throbless
corpse. But not for long. How, one might ask, could
God have permitted this virginal body to corrupt and
decompose, this body from which He had received
life? God in His power and wisdom could not allow
such a thing to happen to His Mother. Besides, it
would hardly have been equitable that she who had
triumphed over sin and the demon by her coredemp-

tive action, should be liable to this, the crowning
punishment of all those inflicted upon our sinful
nature in this life. Even if we had no other assurance
(namely, the assurance of faith), it would be difficult
to believe that this creature, immaculately conceived
and a virgin forever, should have been sullied by the
putrefaction of a corpse in decay. The fact is that the
God of Love, indeed her Son, granted her a miraculous and unprecedented resurrection, in consequence
of which her virginal body was endowed with eternal
youth and unmatched luster. In virtue of this most
marvelous privilege which permitted her to enjoy
beforehand the glories of the resurrection, the
Mother of God is now in heaven in body as well as
in soul, a virgin and mother more beautiful than all
the creatures of the universe.

Now, in the state of blessedness, her soul is wholly
enlightened by the wisdom of the Word. Now, at
last, she beholds forever the presence of God and is
able to adore God in her Son, the Son who is the
eternal thought of the Father. Not only she but also
the other Persons of the Blessed Trinity and all the
blessed are filled with torrents of delight through
beholding in her Son the vision of God. So great is
Mary's glory and blessedness in heaven that it surpasses that of all the angels and saints. No other
creature enjoys such proximity to the three divine
Persons as Mary. Her gaze in heaven reaches to the
inmost depths of the Trinity.

Nothing, moreover, can compare with the splendor found in the assumed body of the Mother of
Jesus. In her, all the qualities of the glorified body
enjoy their highest perfection. Save for the beauty
and divine splendor of Jesus, nothing can match the

splendors of grace possessed by His Mother, the ideal of womanhood, bathed in the beauties and glories of a soul endowed with the vision of God.

Only to see Mary would be enough to make one happy beyond words for all eternity. All the sufferings on earth, yes, all the torments endured by the martyrs of the Church militant would not be too much to pay in return for the privilege of beholding such beauty as hers. One might even say that the Blessed Trinity drew upon all the magnificence at Its command to prepare for Mary the adornments that would befit the Mother of God and make her the masterpiece of the Spirit of Love. The seraphim of heaven had never seen in a creature such marvelous beauty as hers. Through the radiant splendor of her soul, through the external brilliance and luster of her risen body, Mary is the most perfect living image of the Blessed Trinity, the most exalted likeness of the beauty and splendor of Christ.

8   MEDIATRESS BEFORE
THE BLESSED TRINITY

Situated as she is at the summit of creation, in close proximity to her Son and in the very bosom, so to speak, of the Blessed Trinity, the Mother of God occupies, in the divine plan, the role of universal Mediatress. To understand the importance of her role it should be noted that the whole plan of action by which the grace of sanctification is communicated to souls is governed by an inviolable order. In the first place, the Blessed Trinity is the primordial source of all blessings and graces. But all these blessings and graces have been entrusted to Christ, the only Media-

tor between God and men. They are contained, as in
a boundless sea, in the fullness of His grace of headship. Mary, on her part, is the channel through
which Christ brings us all the graces of salvation.
Thus we have the Trinity, the Christ, the Virgin:
this is the order according to which all the spiritual
treasures and blessings vouchsafed by the Deity are
communicated; and these treasures and blessings are
poured forth without cease in the Church of God.[9]

This order has been established by the free determination of divine Wisdom, and by reason of this
determination the basic laws of the economy of salvation have been irrevocably fixed. Hence, not a
single grace is imparted to souls by the Blessed Trinity without passing through the hands of Mary. Such
is the immutable will of Him who was pleased to
make her the repository of all the blessings of God.
What this means is that both in Himself and in His
coming into the souls of men, Jesus Christ is and
ever remains the fruit of the womb of Mary.

Not only do all graces come through Mary, but
she is also the way we must follow in returning to
the Father's house to be made perfect in the unity of
the Trinity. The Church, which is well aware of this,
chooses to go to Christ only through Mary, and the
very saints whom she invokes approach God through
the intercession of Mary. They understand most
clearly that Jesus is never found except with His
Mother, and that only His Mother always has access
to God. She is the Mediatress for all other mediators,

[9] "Every grace that is communicated to this world comes by
a threefold course, being dispensed in most orderly fashion
from God to Christ, from Christ to the Virgin, and from the
Virgin to us" (St. Bernardine of Siena, Sermon VI, *De Annuntiatione*, a. 1, no. 2).

and Mediatress before the one Mediator,[10] and through Him, with Him, and in Him, universal Mediatress before the Blessed Trinity. In sum, Mary brings both God to us and us to God. As, on the one hand, God comes down to us through Mary, so on the other hand must we return to God through Mary.

[10] In the phrase of Leo XIII: "Ad Mediatorem Mediatrix" (*Fidentem,* Sept. 20, 1896).

eight

How the Church Regards Mary

The mind of the Church is filled with thoughts of Mary.

The Church's praise of Mary is expressed in every shape and form that love can devise. The Bible has supplied the basic outlines for her portrait as the Mother of Christ. With these to guide her, the Church has given full rein to the aspirations of her heart. The better to sing the praises of Mary, she has drawn upon all the resources at her command, appealing to her creative genius, to the deepest yearnings of her mystic soul, to all the arts and crafts with their power to stir the heart to praise and admiration.

I   PROPHECIES, FIGURES, AND SYMBOLS

The Church has always preferred to find the true character of the Mother of Jesus in the events relating to the first origins of the human race. Thus we find that from the very beginning she has always regarded Mary as a new Eve, come to restore the supernatural life that was lost by the first woman's sin of pride and disobedience. As the one, so the other has influenced, though in different ways, the destiny of all mankind. Such is the view of Mary taken, for example, by St. Justin, St. Irenaeus, and Tertullian; and as time goes on we find patristic thought epitomizing its belief regarding Mary in this one succinct phrase: "Death from Eve, life from Mary."[1] Indeed, this theme of the new Eve, which is so dear to modern Mariology, sums up perfectly the role that Mary performed in being associated with Christ for the purpose of giving us spiritual birth in the life of God.

In addition to being the new Eve, Mary is a virgin-mother. This unheard-of marvel, also, the Church has always contemplated in awe and admiration. The "almah" of Isaias bringing forth the Emmanuel, this mystery of motherhood with maidenhood, was a theme which the artists of the Middle Ages loved to depict in their cathedrals and churches; and the contemplation of it delighted the heart of a St. Bernard as well as of other medieval saints and doctors. A woman wearing in her crown both jewels of womanhood—both motherhood and maidenhood—this is a glory of which Christianity alone can boast.

Prompted and inspired by the Holy Spirit, the Church found in Sacred Scripture numerous types and figures, living symbols, as it were, of the Mother of God. Thus, Mary is not only the new Eve but also the eternal exemplar of womanhood in all its forms: virgin, wife, mother. In her are found the purity and attractiveness of a Rebecca, the beauty of a Rachel,

[1] "Mors per Evam, vita per Mariam."

the strength of soul of a Judith, and the gentleness with sovereign rule of an Esther.

The figures and symbols of Sacred Scripture signalize the great wealth and variety of the privileges conferred on the Mother of Christ. For example, Mary is the ark of Noe, which weathered the flood tide of sin and the consequent divine wrath, and which harbors those who have been predestined to eternal life. She is the ladder of Jacob, held up by God Himself, which angels ministering to the Most High unceasingly ascend and descend. She is the burning bush of Moses, which symbolizes her inviolable virginity. She is, also, a most beautiful and pure dove, a garden enclosed, a fountain sealed up. She is the gate that shall not be opened except to the Lord God of Israel, the house wisdom has built herself, the temple resplendent with divine grandeur and filled with the glory of the Lord, the city of God the foundations whereof are in the holy mountains, the impregnable tower of strength, the fortress and refuge of the hosts of God, the ark of the covenant.

Besides those just mentioned, the Church found in nature a large array of Marian symbols. Thus, the Mother of God is bright as the morn, a garden of delight, a paradise overflowing the earth with the waters of life. She is by turns the dawn of salvation, the star, the moon, the sun; in the words of the liturgy, she is "fair as the moon, bright as the sun." [2] She is the cloud that dropped down dew from heaven, the virginal earth that brought forth the Saviour. Flowers, trees, fragrances, all the poetry of nature, in fact, is summoned forth to sing the praises of the Virgin Mary.

[2] "Pulchra ut luna, electa ut sol."

Even all this is not enough to extol Mary. The Church goes yet further. Feeling that words of her own can never adequately exalt the sublime grandeur and exquisite beauty of this woman, she introduces into her liturgy the most beautiful texts found in the Sapiential Books and in the Canticle of Canticles. These texts emphasize that at the moment of the creation of the world, in fact from all eternity, Mary was present in the mind of God, figuring in all His works. Yet, wonderful as His works of creation are, the greatest wonder of all was reserved by God for Mary's own soul. It is with this thought in mind that the Church salutes her in the words: "Thou art all fair, O Mary; in thee there is not the stain of original sin." [3]

2 VIRGINAL PURITY

All men, even the greatest sinners among them, love to see in a man or woman the innocence of virginity. The Church on earth, living as she does among sinners, has always venerated the virginal purity and innocence of Mary. For in Mary there is no defilement, nothing impure or unchaste. She is *the* virgin, the virgin whose immaculate beauty shines like a crystal. Since the moment when the angel saluted her as full of grace and purity, resplendent with the splendor of the God who was concealed in her womb, all Christian generations have exalted her as one endowed with inviolable purity. We, men as well as women, have found in Mary a living likeness of the radiant brightness of God Himself, and we are justly proud of this masterpiece of our race, more pure than

[3] "Tota pulchra es, Maria, et macula originalis non est in te."

the angels, worthy to have become the living taber-
nacle of the Word of God.

From the time of the Apostles' Creed down
through the ages, in ancient as well as most modern
melodies, the Christian world has always proclaimed
its faith in the incorruptible and inviolate virginity of
Mary: virgin not only before becoming the Mother of
Jesus, and virgin-mother who bore the eternal God in
her chaste womb, but virgin also after the birth of the
Saviour, virgin forever. It was Christ's glory, and His
alone, to be the Son of the Virgin. This marvel the
Church has memorialized in one of her doxologies,
singing: "Glory be to Thee, O Lord! Virgin-born
Thou wast . . ."[4]

In the simplest motets as well as in more learned
hymns, the Church praises and exalts in Mary this
miraculous preservation of integrity both of soul and
body; for in her, as in all virgins, purity shines first
in the soul before it is reflected in the body. To be
pure and untouched, wholly consecrated to God down
to the last fiber of her being, and yet to be heart and
soul a mother, more mother than any woman ever
was—such is the unique marvel and wonder of Mary.
Christian thought, in fact, never dissociates her virgin-
hood from her motherhood, perceiving as if by instinct
that only virgin motherhood was compatible with
divine motherhood.

The Fathers and the doctors of the Church, also,
found themselves enraptured as they contemplated
this splendor, already glimpsed by Isaias but not fully
manifested until the Church of Jesus could behold
face to face the radiant glory of the Mother of the

[4] "Gloria tibi, Domine,
    Qui natus es de Virgine . . ."

Word. Thus, in her litany of praises the Church proclaims without cease the inviolable purity of Mary, a purity which is above that of any other creature. She is the "Virgin most pure," the "Mother undefiled," the "Queen of virgins," and even the "Queen of angels," so great is the kinship between the virginal beauty of Mary and the shining splendor of the pure spirits. Even the most unperceptive and uninitiated person cannot but notice that in the liturgy of the Church the word "virgin" recurs incessantly whenever she sings the praises and glories of Mary. That is her personal, her private name, as it were. She alone among mankind could say: "I am the Immaculate." She is the Virgin, the Holy Virgin, the most Holy Virgin.

3   DIVINE MOTHERHOOD

Mary's astounding purity and innocence was not an end in itself. Like all of her privileges, it was directed toward her supreme prerogative, her divine motherhood. This unique prerogative places her so far above all creatures as to be beyond comparison, and establishes her in the very order of being where her Incarnate Son is God. Here, then, in the praise of Mary's divine motherhood, the Church's enthusiasm is at its height. Here, in magnifying the holy Mother of God, her ardor is unbounded, whether it be in prayer and song, in the teachings of her doctors, or in the inspirations of her artists and poets. For here she is praising the one whom, on the eve of the proclamation of her divine motherhood, the people of Ephesus jubilantly extolled as the Theotokos, the true Mother of God.

According to St. Thomas, through the grandeur of her divine motherhood Mary touches on the infinite.[5] By reason of this title she occupies a place so near to God as to seem to be suffused, in a manner of speaking, with the uttermost being of the Blessed Trinity. None other than Pope Leo XIII declared, "Beyond all question, the dignity of the Mother of God is so great and sublime that nothing greater could be effected. . . . The Mother of God surpasses in the highest degree all other creatures."[6] Pope Pius XI pronounced her honor and dignity the highest after God.[7] "She is by far more excellent," he said, "than all the angels, more excellent even than the seraphim and cherubim."[8] To these affirmations we could add innumerable passages from the Fathers and the doctors of the Church, all testifying to their faith in this, the most sublime grandeur of Mary. In their writings they extol without end this unique privilege which granted Mary the honor of conceiving the Son of God in the flesh. We do not mean, obviously, that she gave existence to the divine nature of the Word, but that the eternal Word, who is consubstantial with the Father and is also His only Son, became in the flesh the true Son of Mary.

St. John Damascene, for example, has written glowingly of this, as of all privileges and merits of Mary. It was not an ordinary man, he says, whom the

---

[5] See I, 25, 6.

[6] "Certe matris Dei tam in excelso dignitas est, ut nihil fieri maius queat . . . naturis creatis omnibus longissime Deipara antecellit" (*Quamquam pluries,* Aug. 15, 1889).

[7] "Summa post Deum dignitas" (Encyclical *Lux Veritatis, A.A.S.,* Vol. XXIII, 1931, p. 513).

[8] "Ipsa longe excellentior est omnibus angelis, etiam seraphinis et cherubinis" (*Ibid.*).

Virgin brought forth, nor did He come into Mary from the outside, employing her only as passage into the world, but He took from Mary His true human flesh, of the same substance as ours.[9] No human tongue, to echo the same doctor again, nor any angelic intellect will ever be able to express or to praise adequately the greatness of this woman who encompassed in her womb the glory of the Lord; an immeasurable distance will always separate all other servants of God from her who was His Mother.[10] St. John Damascene is not alone in his praise of Mary's glory. In all ages the doctors of the Church have searched and meditated and contemplated this mystery of a woman whose Son was the only-begotten Son of the Father, and who together with her Son restored the order of the universe.

Nothing, then, save God alone, is more exalted than Mary. He gave her His own Son, the Son who is equal with God. In the words of St. Anselm, "The Son He gave to Mary was not one different from His own, but the same. Henceforth He is indissolubly the Son both of God and of Mary. God created the universe, but Mary brought forth God. Almighty God chose to be born of Mary and together with her to restore all things in the world. He who has the power to call forth all things from nothingness, was pleased to restore nothing without Mary." [11] Through the ages the Church will marvel and be filled with wonder as she contemplates this mystery of a God born of a virgin, and proclaims that only a virgin birth befitted a God. As one of the Christmas hymns ex-

[9] See *De Fide Orthod.*, P.G. 94,1027.
[10] See *Orat. I de Dormitione Deip. V.M.*, P.G. 96,700.
[11] *Orat.* 52, P.L. 158,956.

presses it, "Such a birth did God beseem." [12] Further-more, on their part the theologians will always see in Mary's divine motherhood the highest instance, and the primary source, of all the glory and all the privileges and all the graces of Mary.

4 SORROWFUL COMPASSION

From the resplendent heights of the divine mother-hood the Church turns her gaze toward Calvary, where Mary appears more as the sorrowful Mother of men than the glorious Mother of God. Here, on Calvary, all is suffering. The Mother of God is now the Mother of the Crucified. This is the Virgin whom the Church celebrates in the *Stabat Mater*. Ever since the Middle Ages, in fact, the Church has displayed a fervent devotion in honor of the compassion of Our Lady.

Painters and artists, however, did not always follow the Church's example of moderation. Some went to the extreme of depicting Mary as swooning at the foot of the Cross. Such exhibitions, though they may be well intentioned, exceed the limits of propriety, not to say truth. They can hardly be said to carry the Church's stamp of approval; in short, she condemns them as improper. As always, the Church is in a position to know how far our devotion to the Sorrow-ful Mother should go, and we can trust her to keep it in conformity with the true spirit of faith. Certainly, nothing is further from her mind than to detract in any way from the immensity of a sorrow that was "vast as the sea." Yet, even on Golgotha, she discerns in the soul of Mary the Coredemptress a

[12] "Talis decet partus Deum."

fullness of joy,[13] the joy of a mother glad to sacrifice herself for the happiness of her children.

The Church, moreover, encourages her doctors to look upon this suffering of a mother, united with that of Christ, as the source of our salvation. For, as we know, it was not just an ordinary woman who stood at the foot of the Cross at that decisive hour of redemption; it was the Mother of Christ, who by her sorrowful compassion became the Mother of all men. According to St. Albert the Great, "She gave birth to her first-born without any admixture of sorrow; later she brought forth the whole race simultaneously, but through suffering with her Son." [14] It was by sharing His own suffering and being united with His will that Mary became the associate of Christ, and thereby the Coredemptress of the world.

The Church leaves it to the theologians to determine the precise mode and manner of Mary's coredemption. Those who go furthest in this respect

[13] "Plane gaudens" (Pius X, *Ad diem illum,* Feb. 2, 1904).
[14] "Peperit Filium suum primogenitum sine dolore in sua nativitate, postea peperit totam gentem simul in Filii passione" (*Mariale,* q. 150).

Modern Mariology is quite right in devoting much of its efforts to studying the pertinent works of St. Albert the Great, marked as they are by such precise and pregnant passages as the one just quoted, and the following:

"The Blessed Virgin was chosen by the Lord, not to be His menial, but His partner and assistant . . . she is not a servant, but His helper and associate, sharing in the kingdom as she shared in the sufferings for mankind" (*Mariale,* q. 42).

"Even as she was His colleague in the Redemption through her compassion, so would she be the Mother of all through the restoration of mankind; and just as the whole world is under obligation to God by reason of the most sacred Passion, so is it indebted to the Queen of all by reason of her compassion" (*Mariale,* q. 150).

believe—quite properly, it seems—that Mary participated with her Son in the work of redemption not
only as regards the distribution but also the acquisition of all graces. This would seem to be the correct
view, for, as was mentioned earlier, in the economy
of salvation everything depended on the unique act
of Christ on the Cross offering His redemptive sacrifice to His Father. With this saving oblation the
Mother of Jesus united herself with all her heart, sur-
rendering her own rights as mother over this Son
whom she had conceived, brought forth and reared,
and whom she prepared for the task of giving Himself
in ransom for mankind.[15] On this indivisible, theandric act hung the salvation of the world. Despite the
marked simplicity of this act of oblation, its worth
was infinite, being the source of all blessings destined
to flow from the Redemption to all sons of Adam from
the beginning to the end of the world.

What is to be noted here is that Mary was associated with Christ in this aspect of the Redemption,
that is, in the acquisition of graces, though her part
in it was not the same as Christ's. Mary's position
here is that of the first of the redeemed, with the
priority of rank that the special character of her personal redemption gave her. In virtue of this priority
and precedence, her own action possessed redemptive
worth in a degree and manner that is true of no other
creature. This view of Mary's coredemptive compassion in no way detracts from the sovereign and universal efficacy of Christ's Passion. On the contrary,
the coredemptive effect of Mary's action is precisely
the first and foremost result of Christ's Passion and
its most beautiful triumph; indeed, the fact that

[15] See Pius X, *Ad diem illum*, Feb. 2, 1904.

Christ's redemption merited for a simple creature the title of Coredemptress of the world demonstrates and proclaims its omnipotent power as nothing else could.

5 ETERNAL GLORY

Merit summons forth glory and, in varying degree, gives strength and power to one's action. Mary is in heaven. The Church now contemplates the Coredemptress of the world as the Queen of Heaven, *Regina Coeli*. There, close by her Son, she is bathed in the light of glory, being incomparably above all the angels and saints. Her triumph in heaven shines forth in the beauty of her glorified body, but immeasurably more in the splendor of her soul. Alongside of her, all created glory pales and fades. Only God in His infinite splendor surpasses her.

The whole liturgy of the Assumption is intended to proclaim and acclaim this crowning triumph of the Mother of God. On this feast, the most ancient and the most solemn of the Marian cycle, the Church calls upon all her children to rejoice with her in praise of the eternal glory of the "Queen of Heaven." In heaven, on this day, the angels welcomed with joy unbounded their queenly sovereign. Unceasingly, in songs of praise, they offer thanks and glory to God for the blessings so richly bestowed on her; while on earth men emulate them in love and gratitude for her who, though the Mother of God, is their Mother as well.

In the Church of Christ everything is ultimately appraised in the light of eternity. Mary is now in eternity. There, in brightness and glory, united with the Blessed Trinity in the inmost depths of Its being, she exercises in our behalf a power that is in some way unlimited.[16] From the summit of glory where she is enthroned, she watches over the Church and is ever solicitous to bring all nations and all men to the City of God.[17] She is, as we have said again and again, the repository of all graces. All blessings of God come to mankind through her. "God," declared Pope Leo XIII, "has established the fullness of all good in her." [18] Every grace, it is true, has its source in Christ, but Jesus imparts it to us only through Mary; and even as we can go to the Father only through the Son, so only through His Mother can we be united with Christ.[19] All the treasures of the redemption are at her disposal. She rules the world as sovereign, she expiates all our offenses, she reconciles all men with God—in a word, she is the universal Mediatress.

6 THE CULT OF MARY

Mary is the Mother of God. Therein lies the ultimate reason for the cult of hyperdulia, that is, for the special veneration that the Church offers only to the Mother of Christ—and to no other saint. It is a veneration that far surpasses every devotion offered to the saints of the Church. As we know, in her forms of

[16] See Leo XIII, *Adjutricem populi*, Sept. 5, 1895.
[17] As Leo XIII wrote: "Dispensing, as Mediatress with God, the graces of heaven, Mary enjoys the highest rank of power and glory in heaven, so that she might bestow upon men the help of her protection as they strive most earnestly, amid so many difficulties and dangers, to attain the heavenly city above" (*Supremi Apostolatus*, Sept. 1, 1883).
[18] "In qua totius boni posuit plenitudinem" (*Ibid.*).
[19] See Leo XIII, *Octobri mense*, Sept. 22, 1891.

worship and devotion the Church reveals her deepest thoughts and aspirations, since prayer expresses the life of the soul. To know what fills her heart one must see the Church at prayer.

Accordingly, it is noteworthy that the liturgical prayer of the Church abounds with thoughts, reflections and meditations on Mary. Next to the Blessed Trinity and the Person of Christ, the mystery of Mary is uppermost in the thought and contemplation of the Church. The Church simply cannot bring herself to dissociate the mysteries of the Mother from those of the Son. Christmas, Epiphany, the Seven Sorrows, Easter, Pentecost—all, as if one feast, extol the Saviour and His Mother together. Besides these, there are other, more personal, feasts of our Lady distributed throughout the liturgical year, from the feast of the Immaculate Conception to that of her glorious Assumption. Furthermore, not only in the liturgy but in other domains of Christian culture as well, Mary has moved her children to praise and admiration. It was devotion to Mary that built some of our most beautiful cathedrals, and inspired poets and artists to produce some of the most beautiful masterpieces in Christian art and literature.

To speak truly, the whole life of the Christian is motivated and inspired not only by his strictly liturgical worship but also by his devotion to Mary. In fact, this devotion is only an extension of his liturgical worship and is integrally related to it. At home, mothers teach their little children to pray with confidence to the Mother of Jesus. To her the young woman entrusts her purity, the growing youth his future; and the man in his prime, wearied by the false hopes and hard knocks of life, also comes beseeching before the presence of this woman ever pure and, mother that she is, ever accessible. And at the end of life, the last look of the dying will be to Mary, for the smile of mercy that will open to him the gates of heaven.

It is a matter of human experience that, to whatever depths he may have sunk, a man always clings to one hope: his mother. To her he always looks with confidence. In the Church of Christ even the most wretched sinner knows that he can always count on the mercy and goodness of her who is the "Refuge of Sinners." Who, for example, does not know the poignant cries of the unfortunate Verlaine, whose experience ran the gamut of human misery and affliction? He wanted in the end no other love than Mary his Mother, no other memory but Mary.[20] His wish was to die with Mary at his side.[21] In that wish all children of Mary join with all their heart.

[20] See Verlaine, *Sagesse,* II.
[21] *Angelus de Midi.*

nine

"Behold Thy Mother!"

Since Mary is our Mother, may we give her the heart and love of a child.

In Christianity everything holds together. The teachings of dogma lay the foundations for the teachings of morality. Consequently, the mystery of Mary itself indicates what our practical conduct should be in regard to the Mother of God. As we have seen, her unique position at the very center of all the great mysteries of Christianity merits her a special veneration, embodying gratitude, love, and admiration. For it is she who is never invoked in vain; it is she who, as His Mother, is privileged to have at her command the God of the universe, and she who keeps watch over every human being with the tender affection of a mother.

Jesus Himself has given us the key to the mystery of Mary. He who is both the Truth and the Son of Mary, who created her by His divine power, who made her His associate in the entire work of redemption; He who knows her best, knows her in fact with infinite knowledge, before dying He spoke the decisive words that sum up the essential nature of the mystery of Mary, namely, "Behold thy mother!" Mary indeed is all mother: His and ours. In this respect, as in others, we are to be but one with Him, loving His Mother as He, venerating her as He, that is, with the heart and love of a son. For we are her sons. Jesus Himself had indicated as much in the words "Behold thy son." He said in effect: "Mother, behold thy children. Acknowledge every one of My brethren as a son of yours."

We see, then, that the tragedy of Golgotha, which has given us the ultimate explanation on earth regarding so many things, has also given us the deepest insight as to what should be our relation to the Mother of God. It is all summed up in this: she is our Mother, we are her children. "Behold thy mother, behold thy son." [1] In these words from Christ on the Cross the mystery of Mary is unfolded beyond all doubt and dispute.

I SPIRITUAL MOTHERHOOD

All motherhood involves three principal functions. A mother conceives, gives birth to, and brings up her children until they are grown men and women. Mary performed all of these offices. By her fiat she conceived us at the moment of the Incarnation; at the foot of the Cross she gave us spiritual birth; and from heaven she continues her task of nurturing us unto our final perfection in God. As said earlier, it is not the transitory life of man that she gives us, as our mothers on earth do, but a divine life, life eternal. She conceived us at the same time as she conceived the Son of the eternal God, and this spiritual mother-

[1] See John 19:26-27.

hood bears the indelible mark of its divine origin. She loves us with the same love she has for her Son, and she wants us to share with Him and her the same intimate life of fellowship they have with the Father. Both her spiritual and her divine motherhood are wholly centered in the Blessed Trinity.

It was one and the same impulse of love that moved her to become the Mother of the Saviour and our Mother, in other words, the Mother of the total Christ. As a matter of fact, the indissoluble unity of Christ's mystical body made such a coincidence of love inevitable. It is incredible, therefore, that she should have conceived the head without the members. Her spiritual motherhood was intended to accomplish the same end as her divine motherhood, namely, to make us perfect in unity with the Father and the Son, to give us by grace what the Son possesses by nature. Thus, the grandeur of her divine motherhood also sheds the clearest possible light on the significance of her spiritual motherhood. It is by the same life-giving bonds that we are united both with the Mother and the Son. Consequently, the two motherhoods and the two sonships, that is, Christ's and ours, throw mutual light on each other. Our divine sonship by grace has its origin in the eternal sonship of the Word, the source and exemplar of our sonship.

To repeat, the virgin of the Incarnation, Mother of God and of men, loves us with the same love she has for her Son, and through Him and with Him she seeks to bring us into intimate union and fellowship with the Father. In her virginal womb, as also in the eternal bosom of the Father, dwelled both the only-begotten Son and His entire mystical body. The very life of the Word came to live in her so that she might communicate it to the world. Hence her spiritual motherhood, even as her divine motherhood, of which the former is an extension, brings her whole life and being in relation with the Blessed Trinity.

It is difficult for us to comprehend how great was the love with which the young Mother of God, from the first day of the Incarnation, clasped all men to her heart, so to speak. It is more than mere rhetoric to say that from the fiat of the Incarnation to the fiat on Calvary she was constantly in the pangs of spiritual childbirth, reaching their culmination at the foot of the Cross. At that hour of her coredemption she wrested us from the clutches of death and gave us birth unto new life. We see, therefore, why Jesus should have chosen this solemn moment to proclaim to all the world the spiritual motherhood of Mary. For, the death of Jesus, which was offered up by our Mother, marks the exact moment of our coming into new life, the life of God.

The highest and most sublime function of a mother is to lift up the souls of her children to God. This is true of Mary par excellence. Now, after her glorious Assumption, Mary continues to be the vigilant mother, solicitous for all her children, seeking to bring them the life itself of the Blessed Trinity. From baptism on, she, like Christ, accompanies us in the various stages of our spiritual life. Through her intervention as Mediatress she provides for all our wants, since a mother's watch and care extend to all the needs of her children. With a mother's solicitude Mary obtains for us both material and spiritual helps to fulfill the needs of body and soul. She enlightens our understanding by the inspirations of faith and strengthens our will by the communication of grace.

She curbs the unruliness of the senses and protects us in whatever social environment we may find ourselves by trade or profession, for man must achieve his eternal destiny by living and working with others. Moreover, all the angels of God are at Mary's service to secure the happiness of the elect. She controls all events of history, all powers of the universe, to the end that she may bring all her children to the City of God. Her mission as mother is to form Christ in souls and to complete our conformation to the image of the Son.[2]

2   LIFE IN MARY

Since Mary is our Mother, we ought to go to her with the heart of a child. No need, here, of precise formula or complicated method. The more simple one's spiritual life, the more divine it is. Unhappily, this is not always so well understood as it ought to be. It is not unusual to find certain individuals who are greatly distressed because they cannot *feel* their devotion to the Blessed Mother. And so they are driven almost to despair, thinking themselves to be lacking in love. All this fret and worry is unnecessary, to say the least. Such individuals should stop being worried. Let them rest assured that devotion need not be *felt*. The ways of God are infinitely varied. Every soul must follow, freely and in all earnestness, the form of devotion that nature and temperament impose. Our particular form of intimate affection for Mary should be mirrored in, and be expressive of, our personality. In the saints, the cult of Mary always reflects the basic features of their spirituality.

[2] See Romans 8:29.

Nevertheless, after all is said and done, there remain two great providential laws in the economy of salvation, and in order to advance on the way to divine union all Christian souls must conform to them. In the first place, our spiritual life must be centered in Christ; but, and this is the second point, it will be more perfect in proportion as it develops and grows under the influence of Mary. This does not mean just mumbling a few quick prayers every day. Indeed not. Our recourse to Mary has to come from the heart, and it has to be regular and persistent. In times of great decision or difficulty it is natural enough for us to look to Mary, but we ought to bring her our joys and expectations as well as our sorrows and adversities. Then, if we have confidence in her, prayer to Mary will obtain all things. She is at all times our Mother, from the cradle to the grave—and beyond. At the beginning of life, on the day of baptism, it was she who conveyed to each of us the title of child of God; at the end of life, it is she who will open to us the gates of heaven.

Such regular and persistent recourse to Mary leads to a state of abiding and uninterrupted communion with her. Happy those who have learned the secret of living in Mary and for whom, in the words of St. Ambrose, Mary has become the soul of their soul.[3] To possess this secret of living wholly in Mary betokens a grace of predilection. For such privileged souls the Mother of Christ becomes the all-pervading influence of their lives. They live and move only in Mary. Echoing the famous words of St. Paul, they

---

[3] "May the soul of Mary be in each of us, so as to magnify the Lord, and may the spirit of Mary be in each of us, so as to rejoice in God" (*Expositio in Luc.*, Bk. II, no. 26).

can truly say: "For me to live in Mary, the better to live in Christ and in the Blessed Trinity." [4]

Yet Mary is not an end in herself, but a means of coming to Christ. She is, however, the best and quickest means of coming to Him and, through Him, to the Blessed Trinity; for it is in the Trinity that all is made perfect in the unity of the Father and the Son together with the Spirit proceeding from both. Instead of being an obstacle, Mary is in fact the most direct way to Christ and, through Him, to the Father. She is, in a manner of speaking, the short-cut to the Blessed Trinity.

In many things in life, it is each to his own taste. Within limits this also applies in choosing our particular form of devotion to Mary. Each one should feel free to follow the way he prefers, or the way he has been taught by the order or community in which his vocation lies, or the way he has learned from some other authentic teacher, depending upon his state of life. The phrase "bondage of love" expresses admirably one point of view as regards devotion to Mary, but it is not necessarily suited to everybody. Living the rosary is another excellent way of loving and honoring Mary. Repeating, prayerfully, the Hail Mary, and meditating on the principal mysteries of Christ, soon puts the soul in an atmosphere that is divine. Through such means the soul quickly learns how to live habitually in the presence of the Blessed Trinity. [5]

[4] See Philippians 1:21. St. Peter Damian expresses this thought as follows: "Everything through her and in her and with her" (Sermon II, *De Annuntiatione B.V.M., P.L.* 144,558).
[5] See Theological Note XI, p. 150.

Some religious communities, on the other hand, prefer a form of spirituality that is more strictly liturgical and somewhat less given to special exercises in regard to Mary. This is as it should be. The Church is universal enough to contain such variety. Besides, any form of Christian holiness or perfection is only a particular and limited expression of the infinite fullness of Christ's grace of headship and of the supereminent perfection of the Mother of God, queen and exemplar of all saints.

The fact is that, however much we may consider and contemplate the mystery of Mary, we shall never comprehend its true immensity. Its real dimensions lie above mere human horizons and can be glimpsed only by the divine light of God's revelation. God has revealed to mankind the pre-eminent place that Mary occupies in the arrangement and government of this vast universe—it is a place that is next to Christ.

Let us recall briefly where Mary stands in the eternal plan of God. As we have seen, God the Father, loving us with His eternal love, took mercy on sinful man and decreed to send His Son so that we might share in His own life. Such being God's will, it was necessary to provide a mother for His Son become flesh. God chose Mary. Not only men, however, but also the angels were called to become intimate members of the family of the three divine Persons, to be made perfect in the same unity with the Father, the Son, and the Spirit of Love. This final consummation in the Trinity is the whole end and purpose of the creation of the world and of the mysteries of salvation. From the point of view of mankind, God created the whole universe of spiritual and material beings, and then sent His only Son into the world for no other reason than to lead us to the intuitive contemplation of the inmost life of the Blessed Trinity.

This, too, is the ultimate purpose of the mystery of Mary, namely, to establish souls in the life of the Trinity. God the Father, who has made us His children, wants us to be conformed to the image of His only-begotten Son and to be vivified by His own Spirit of Love. But for God's family of adoption, even as for His Son, the Word Incarnate, a mother was necessary. To be our mother, God gave us the Mother of His own Son. Therein lies the substance of Mary's role. Without her we should be orphans; divine Wisdom knew it. Hence the reason why, in the present order of providence, all who are children of God are, like Jesus Himself, sons of Mary as well. Hence, also, why no one can have God for Father who does not have Mary for Mother.

On the morning of the Resurrection Jesus Himself, having reconciled us with God, was pleased to declare how much he regarded us as His brothers. Appearing to Mary Magdalene, He admonished her, "Go to my brethren and say to them, 'I ascend to my Father and your Father, to my God and your God.'" [6] And the Apostle John, to whom Jesus entrusted His Mother at the foot of the Cross, does not hesitate to say that on earth it is impossible for us to realize how much God has loved us, "that we should be called children of God; and such we are." [7] There will come a day, however, when we shall see and understand, and when all shadows and obscurities will be removed;

[6] John 20:17.
[7] I John 3:1.

when, in other words, "we shall see him just as he is." [8]

On that day, when the sun will have set to rise no more and all men are gathered together for the last judgment, the unbelieving and sinful nations, seeing Him whom they pierced,[9] will tremble in terror. Then, He who was crucified on Golgotha will appear in all His majesty. And as He turns to the elect, we shall hear the same voice that was heard on Calvary, saying to us, not in the tragic tone of one in agony, but in the triumphant tone of the Saviour of the world: "Blessed of My Father, see and behold your Mother!" In that instant, Son that He is, He will honor His Mother finally and forever. He will reveal to us, in the full light of eternity, a woman shining with beauty and glory, her golden crown set in brilliant stars, the woman whom by her character and countenance we, together with Him, shall recognize as our true, our common Mother.

[8] I John 3:2.
[9] See Apocalypse 1:7.

ten

To My Mother: Mary

I want to live and die with the rosary in my hands.

O Mother of the Word, from all eternity the divine and most Blessed Trinity has reposed in you Its love and contemplation. At the earliest dawn of history, we find you promised and announced in advance as the Woman surrounded in mystery, victress over the demon, vanquishing all evil, triumphing over all the enemies of God.

Later, the greatest of the prophets marveled and wondered as he saw you in prophetic vision, appearing now in the shining purity of your virginal conception, O Mother of the Emmanuel. Come upon this sinful earth of ours, you stood resplendent and immaculate as the lily, without the stain of original sin, clothed in marvelous beauty, full of grace, the masterpiece of God.

Yet this fullness of grace was to be only the beginning, the first step toward that most exalted and stupendous marvel, your divine motherhood; for by this you were raised aloft to the sublime heights of uncreated life in the Blessed Trinity, even to sharing with God the Father the possession of the same Son.

Thenceforth your mystery unfolded in all its vastness, establishing you in kinship with all the Trinity, being Handmaid of the Father, Mother of the Son, and Spouse of the Holy Spirit, sharing in all the works of God, the "complement of the Trinity."

But this is not all. The light of God's revelation also permits me to see in you the countenance of my Mother, at once the most divine and the most human of mothers, wholly consecrated to God's Son, and wholly devoted also to the happiness of His poor, wretched children. In you all is splendor and shining brightness; in you, the glow of love that is pure; in you, sorrowful compassion over the unhappy lot of your afflicted children. Yet, the more revolting our defilements, the more gloriously proclaimed are you as the Mother of Mercy. My sins, far from turning me from your purity and holiness, from the fullness of your grace and the exalted grandeur of your divine motherhood, my sins, I say—yes, my innumerable sins —rather strengthen me in my boldness to come to you. For, is it not for my sins that you are the Mother of God?

Now, amid the splendors of glory, you hold sway from your throne in heaven. In your watchful care no one is forgotten, nothing overlooked. With a mother's heart and affection you look after the Church and after all your children. Your power is unlimited, since God's own omnipotence is in your hands to dispose of at your good pleasure. Keep us, then, from all evil. Keep the Church true to her divine mission among the nations. Strengthen her in her daily struggles. Grant her to be strong and unyielding in battle for the triumph of Christ. May heroism and holiness abound in her, so as to build up speedily the eternal City of God.

As for myself, extend your loving care over me, sinner that I am; and for the sake of the blood of your Son, obtain in your great mercy the pardon of all my sins. No longer will I suffer my wretchedness and weakness to dismay me, for I know that you, my Mother, are the Mother of God, and that I am rich with all the riches of your Son. For the sake of the greater honor and glory of God, whose Mother you are, grant that I may become holy with the very holiness of God, and that my life may shine with the light of His splendor, and that I may be conformed to the image of your first-born Son. Give my soul lasting abode in the immutable Trinity. And grant, I pray, that from now on I may be steadfast in love that is pure, and live only for the greater glory of your Son. I want to spend my life loving you, sounding your praises . . .

Then, when I shall have breathed my last, and my lips have whispered your name for the last time on earth, bring me forthwith to the full light of glory. There, together with the Word and you, I shall praise forever the eternal glory of the all-merciful and all-adorable Blessed Trinity.

Theological Notes

I. THE DIVINE MOTHERHOOD, THE KEY-STONE OF MARIAN THEOLOGY

In a most valuable passage from one of Pope Pius XI's encyclicals, the methodological role that the divine motherhood occupies in the structure of Mariological science is clearly set forth. From this passage it is evident that the directive principles and axioms of Mariology, and the conclusions drawn from them, all depend on the divine motherhood as on a first principle. The Pope wrote as follows:

"From the dogma of the divine motherhood emanate, as from a deep and hidden spring, both Mary's unprecedented grace and her pre-eminent rank, which is second only to that of God. Indeed, as Aquinas admirably remarks, 'By reason of being the Mother of God the Blessed Virgin possesses, in a way, an infinite dignity resulting from the infinite good which is God' (I, 25, 6, ad 4). This same thought is stated and explained in greater detail by Cornelius a Lapide (*In Mt.* 1:6) as follows: 'The Blessed Virgin is the Mother of God; therefore she excels by far all the angels, even the seraphim and the cherubim. She is the Mother of God; therefore she is most pure and most holy, so much so that aside from God no greater purity is conceivable. She is the Mother of God;

therefore whatever favor or privilege has been granted to any of the saints, she has received above all others'" (*Lux Veritatis, A.A.S.,* Vol. XXIII, 1931, p. 513).

This paragraph indicates the correct method to be followed in the systematic study of Mary, namely, to relate everything to her divine motherhood:

1   First, the Pope points out the highest source of all Mary's greatness, namely, the dogma of the divine motherhood.

2   Secondly, he shows that the following privileges of Mary depend on her divine motherhood: *a*) her place at the summit of creation, second only to God; *b*) her being incomparably more exalted than all the angels, including the seraphim and cherubim; *c*) her unprecedented fullness of grace; *d*) her being pure and holy in the highest degree.

3   Lastly, he shows that the Mariological axioms also are based on the fact of the divine motherhood.

The science of theology could hardly have failed to give the strongest emphasis to this capital point, namely, that the whole body of Mariology is based on the divine motherhood. Thus we have from Suarez this profound observation: "Her dignity as the Mother of God is compared to other created graces as a *first form* to its properties; and, conversely, other graces are compared to this dignity as dispositions to the form. Accordingly, this dignity of mother is more excellent, even as the form is more perfect than its properties and dispositions" (*In III partem D. Thomae,* Q. 27, Disp. I, sect. 2; Vivès ed. Vol. XIX, p. 9).

In his excellent treatise on Mariology, Merkelbach has succeeded in bringing the light of this cardinal principle to bear on all his conclusions. He writes:

"That Mary is absolutely immaculate, full of grace and glory; that she was and is a virgin forever, associated with Christ; that she is the new Eve, our spiritual Mother, and Mediatress between God and men— all this has its source and foundation in the fact that she was destined to be, and in due time became, the Mother of God. Therefore, by saying that Mariology treats of the Mother of God the Redeemer, the whole doctrine of Mary and all her privileges are sufficiently indicated from the precise point of view under which they are to be treated by sacred science. Mariology, then, is the *science of the Mother of God,* and, indeed, in the present order of salvation, of God the Redeemer.

"The divine motherhood, therefore, is the crown of Mary's dignity, of her pre-eminence and supernatural exaltation; it is the principle, the source, and the measure of her holiness and graces both in the past and in the future; it is the basis of all her relationships with us, the source also and the strength of her love for us. And on our part it is the foundation and reason for perpetual gratitude, love and devotion. Hence, the divine motherhood defines her essential nature and is the source and measure of her holiness, of her attributes, privileges and power; it is the center of all her prerogatives."

In short, as regards Mariology the divine motherhood is the principle and the measure of everything. Worthy of mention here is the *Florilegium mariale* containing many passages on this primacy of the divine motherhood, which Keuppens had the happy thought to append to his *Mariologiae compendium.* Much to be desired in this connection is an *Enchiridion mariale,* which would bring together in one volume the finest passages on the subject from the Fathers of the Church and from theological tradition. Such a work would render inestimable service.

II. REGARDING A SCIENTIFIC ORDER FOR MARIOLOGY

In recent years research has given us a number of excellent, scholarly studies on the Mariology of various Fathers and doctors of the Church. There have been, for example, studies on the Mariology of St. Irenaeus, St. Jerome, St. Augustine, St. John Damascene, St. Albert the Great, St. Alphonse de Liguori, and many others. This more or less historical approach has been paralleled, also, by efforts to arrive at a systematic organization of the science of Mariology.

It seems to use that in following the methodological insight displayed by St. Thomas in his Christology, it is possible to build up a rigorously coherent body of Mariological science. In such a study the divine motherhood would have the same pivotal role as the hypostatic union in the mystery of Christ. In Mariology everything, both in the order of being and in the order of operation, has to be built around the definition of the mystery of Mary, which is that Mary is the Mother of a Saviour-God.

In the light of experience gained from teaching Mariology on several occasions, may we suggest the broad outlines of a plan that we have found preferable. As can be seen, we would divide the study of the mystery of Mary into two major parts, following the distinction between the order of being and the order of operation, as we have it in the treatise on the mystery of Christ.

(A)

The scientific study based on causes.

1   The *leitmotiv of the divine motherhood* and Mary's predestination, viewed against the background of a redemptive Incarnation. Mary is the Mother of a Saviour-God, to accomplish a work whose end is mercy: "Mater misericordiae." This is the highest view of the mystery of Mary that wisdom can discern.

2   The *essential nature of the divine motherhood* and its connection with the hypostatic order. This is the formal, the most central, aspect of Mariology.

3   The *consequences of the divine motherhood: a)* in regard to God: special relationships with the most Blessed Trinity; *b)* in regard to Christ: the associate of Christ, the new Eve, the Coredemptress of the world (by the principle of association); *c)* in regard to us: spiritual motherhood; *d)* in itself: various perfections, namely, fullness of grace, fullness of knowledge, fullness of power, other privileges. Human limitations of the Mother of Christ (nescience,[1] capacity to suffer, death).

By way of *conclusion:* the universal Mediatress (which sums up the whole mystery, even as the whole mystery of Christ is summed up in the name "Mediator").

(B)

The great acts of mediation in the life of Mary.

Here it would be a question of following the principal mysteries of the economy of salvation as they relate to the Mother of Christ and as they were successively unfolded in history according to God's providence. This would be done without appealing to

[1] See p. 89, note 6.—Translator's note.

insight and understanding that is strictly or specifically theological.

Thus, after having mentioned the prophecies of the Old Testament bearing on Mary, it would be sufficient to consider, as presented in the gospel, the great acts of the Mother of God in behalf of mankind, namely: the fiat at the Incarnation, her coredemptive compassion at the foot of the Cross, her mediatory activity in heaven, taking care at the same time to distinguish the two separate aspects of *acquisition* and *distribution* of all graces of salvation.

Then, as general conclusion: the *cult of Mary*, comprising a study of the cult of hyperdulia and the various devotions to Mary that are found in the Church.

III. MARIAN AXIOMS

It is well known that modern Mariology makes constant use of the Marian axioms, though not always without excess and exaggeration. Be that as it may, tradition does sanction their use, and their essential import may be stated as follows:

1   The axiom of *fittingness.*—According to this axiom we are to attribute to Mary all perfections and all graces and privileges she required for her double office as Mother of God and of men. This is the most basic axiom. Its validity is justified by the principle of finality. In other words, God, in a manner of speaking, owed it to Mary—as He owes it to every creature—to give her all the graces of state that she needed for her work, namely, for her universal role in the economy of salvation. As St. Thomas observes: "When God chooses any persons for some work, He

prepares and disposes them in such a way as to be qualified for the work for which they are chosen" (III, 27, 4c).

Accordingly, the Mother of Christ received in superabundant measure all graces, all natural and supernatural perfections, and all special helps she needed in view of her divine motherhood and her office as Coredemptress of the world.

2 The axiom of *conformity with Christ.*—In virtue of this axiom we attribute to the Coredemptress, not in the same degree but in due proportion, the graces and privileges possessed by the Redeemer, with the exception of those that are the exclusive consequence of His hypostatic union. This axiom has its source in the principle of association.

St. Lawrence of Brindisi has given us an excellent statement of it as follows: "Mary, I say, resembles Christ in every way, as the moon resembles the sun, and Eve resembles Adam. She resembles Him in predestination, in vocation, in justification, in glorification. Christ is seated at the right hand of God, king and highest ruler over all the angels; and Mary is seated at the right hand of God, sovereign queen and mistress of heaven and the angels" (*Super "Fundamenta ejus," Sermo* 2).

3 The axiom of *pre-eminence* and *transcendence.*—This axiom means that all graces and charismatic gifts granted to other saints were received by the Mother of God to a supereminent degree. This is the axiom that is made use of most often, but it must be applied with great discretion. We find it frequently stated in the Fathers and doctors of the Church. Thus, St. Bernard writes: "Whatever, then, is known to have been granted to mortals, even but to the few

and select, it would certainly be improper to think that it was denied to this, so great a virgin, through whom all human beings came forth unto life" (*Epistola 174, P.L.* 182, 334).

St. Thomas speaks in the same vein: "It is reasonable to believe that she who brought forth the only-begotten Son of the Father, full of grace and truth, received greater privileges of grace than all others" (III, 27, 1c).

As we have seen, the Church in her magisterium has adopted this way of speaking of Mary. In one of his encyclicals Pope Pius XI quotes with approval the following passage from Cornelius a Lapide: "She is the Mother of God; therefore whatever favor or privilege has been granted to any of the saints, she has received above all others" (*Lux Veritatis, A.A.S.,* Vol. XXIII, 1931, p. 513).

IV. THE NEW EVE

The oldest form we find in tradition to represent the coredemption of Mary is the parallelism, perhaps we should say the antithetical parallelism, between Mary and Eve. This theme is the key to all present-day problems regarding Mary's universal mediation. It is here that the famous principle of association, so dear to modern Mariology, receives the widest application. In fact, this principle has received so much emphasis from different studies on Mary that in practice the highest principle of all, namely, the divine motherhood, is not given the dominant place it deserves. As for the principle of association and the Mary-Eve parallelism, there is no need here to dwell on the classical passages in St. Justin, Tertullian, and especially St. Irenaeus, passages that testify to its validity and antiquity. Next to the dogma of the divine motherhood, this theme contrasting Eve and Mary is most fundamental.

V. THE DOGMA OF THE IMMACULATE CONCEPTION AND ITS CONSEQUENCES

The historical and doctrinal importance of the dogma of the Immaculate Conception is truly incalculable. Its definition marks the term of a long development in Christian thought and begins a new doctrinal epoch regarding Mary, one in which impetus was given to the full pursuit of Marian studies and devotion. Various pontifical documents, such as those of Pius IX, Leo XIII, and Pius X, have given the cult of Mary and the corresponding theological study a magnificent increase of scope and depth. Well known, of course, is the celebrated dogmatic definition of Pius IX: "We declare, proclaim, and define that this dogma is revealed by God [*formally contained in the deposit of revelation*] and therefore to be firmly and steadfastly believed by all the faithful [*object of divine faith, hence its denial entails heresy*], namely, the dogma which holds that the most Blessed Virgin Mary [*her very person*], from the first moment of her conception [*the exact moment*], by a singular grace and privilege from almighty God [*an exceptional privilege*] and in view of the merits of Jesus Christ the Saviour of the human race [*hence, as one redeemed*], was kept free [*the specific manner of her preventive redemption*] from every stain of original sin [*the precise object of the privilege*]."

This basic formula of faith determines precisely the

object, the *subject,* the *manner,* the *certainty,* and the *exceptional character* of the privilege; moreover, as is seen from the preambles to the definition, it also declares its highest ground and justification, namely, the divine motherhood, which is the keystone on which all the privileges of Mary depend.

Sometimes the privilege of the Immaculate Conception is represented as a restoration, pure and simple, of the state of innocence and primitive justice. This is correct, in a way, as far as Mary's soul is concerned. The privilege of having been conceived immaculate removed from her, as a consequence, all seat of sin and all the disharmony and disequilibrium brought on our nature by the sin of Adam. Accordingly: in her understanding there is neither error nor ignorance, but only nescience;[1] in her will there is neither malice nor inclination to evil; in her sense nature there is neither concupiscence nor evil tendencies, but sinlessness and even impeccability.

On the other hand, this exceptional privilege did not restore the preternatural gifts of impassibility and immortality. The Immaculate remained subject to suffering and death, not as punishment for her personal sins, for she had none, but as part of her human nature.

VI. MARY'S INCOMPARABLE FULLNESS OF GRACE

In particular, two passages of the Bull *Ineffabilis Deus* contain an excellent statement of the mind of the Church regarding the Mother of God's incomparable fullness of grace and her supereminent holiness:

[1] See p. 89, note 6.—Translator's note.

"The ineffable God, whose ways are mercy and truth, whose will is omnipotence, whose wisdom reaches from end to end mightily and ordereth all things sweetly, having foreseen from all eternity the most sorrowful ruin that was to come upon the whole human race from the sin of Adam, had decreed according to the mystery hidden through all the ages to accomplish, by a mystery even more hidden, the first work of His goodness in the incarnation of the Word, so that man, who was led into sin by the cunning of the devil's wickedness, would not utterly perish and undo His most merciful purpose; thus, too, the loss that was to be suffered in the first Adam would be repaired in a manner even more wonderful in the second. Accordingly, from the beginning and before time was, He chose and destined for His only-begotten Son a mother of whom, having been made flesh, He would be born in the blessed fullness of time; and He loved her above all creatures to such a degree as to find in her as in no other His highest complacence. Wherefore, out of the inexhaustible riches of His divinity He lavished upon her, far more than upon all the angels and saints, such an abundance of every heavenly gift and grace that, being always utterly free of every stain of sin and all beautiful and perfect, she was adorned with such fullness of innocence and holiness that aside from God no greater holiness and innocence is conceivable; and in fact, no mind except that of God Himself can comprehend it."

In a further passage of the same Bull the Pope continues as follows: "The Fathers and other writers of the Church meditated deeply on the words of the Angel Gabriel in which he announced to the most Blessed Virgin her most sublime dignity of Mother of God; and they believed that it was in the name of God Himself and at His behest that the Angel called her 'full of grace.' Hence, they taught that by this singular and solemn salutation, never heard before or since, the Mother of God was declared to be the seat of all divine graces, adorned with all the graces and charismatic gifts of the divine Spirit, in fact, was shown to be the almost infinite repository, the inexhaustible abyss, of these same graces, so much so that, never having been subject to the universal curse but rather sharing with the Son in perpetual benediction, she merited to hear from Elizabeth the words that the Holy Spirit moved her to say, namely: 'Blessed art thou among women and blessed is the fruit of thy womb.' Hence, it is their opinion, which is as laudatory as it is unanimous, that the most glorious Virgin, unto whom He who is mighty has done great things, shone forth with such effusion of all heavenly gifts, with such fullness of grace and such holiness as to be, so to speak, an ineffable miracle of God, and indeed as the crown of all miracles, a worthy Mother of God. And therefore, as far as possible for a creature, her excellence approaches that of God Himself, and she surpasses all the praises of heaven and earth, of angels and men."

VII.   THE PRIMARY IMPORTANCE OF THE FIAT OF THE INCARNATION

The more one reflects on the mystery of Mary, the more one becomes aware that her fiat at the incarnation, from which came the redemption of the world, embodied everything, the whole mystery. And one understands, also, the paramount importance that the

Christian tradition from the beginning has attached to it. Well known are the classical texts on this point in St. Justin, in St. Irenaeus and in Tertullian, texts that base Mary's entire role in the economy of salvation on her fiat. A passage from one of St. Bernard's homilies on the words "Missus est" is justly celebrated:

"The Angel awaits the answer, for the moment is at hand when he must return to God who sent him. And we, too, O Queen, are awaiting the word of compassion, we who are weighted down by the sentence of damnation, leaving us wretched. Behold the price of our salvation is being offered to you; if you give your consent, we shall be freed at once. By the eternal word of God we were made, yet behold we die. By your brief answer we are to be recreated, so as to be restored to life. This, O loving Virgin, this, Adam in his sorrow entreats of you . . . this, Abraham and David, too, implore. This also the holy men of old, your ancestors no less, earnestly beg, they who themselves dwell in the valley of the shadow of death. This, in fact, the whole world on bended knee before you is awaiting.

"And it is not without reason they await your reply, for on your word depends consolation for the wretched, redemption for those in bondage, deliverance for the condemned; in short, salvation for all the sons of Adam, that is to say, for all your offspring. O Virgin, give your answer quickly. Speak, O Queen, speak the word which the living on earth, the dead below, and the angels above, all are awaiting" (*Super "Missus est,"* IV, *P.L.* 183, 83).

Pope Pius X, hearkening back to the teaching of Blessed Grignon de Montfort as well as to a splendid

passage in St. Augustine, was most anxious to remind
the Church that at the moment of her fiat Mary became not only the Mother of God, but also our
Mother. He wrote:

"Is not Mary the Mother of Christ? Therefore, she
is also our Mother. For everyone ought to keep it
firmly impressed on his mind that Jesus, who is the
Word made flesh, is also the Saviour of the human
race. Now, as the God-man He received a real, material body, like other men; but as the restorer of our
race He possesses a body that is, so to speak, spiritual
and, as they say, mystical, this body consisting of
those who believe in Christ. The many are one body
in Christ (Rom. 2:6). The Virgin conceived the
eternal Son of God not only so that He might become
man, receiving from her His human nature, but also
that through the nature received from her He might
be the Saviour. For this reason it was that the Angel
announced to the shepherds: 'There has been born to
you today . . . a Saviour, who is Christ the Lord'
(Lk. 2:11).

"Thus, in one and the same womb of His most
chaste Mother, Christ both took His human flesh and
joined to it a spiritual body, consisting of those who
were to believe in Him. Accordingly, *Mary, who bore
the Saviour in her womb, can also be said to have
borne all those whose life was contained in the life
of the Saviour.* Hence, all of us who are united with
Christ, in other words, all who, as the Apostle says,
are members of His body, made from His flesh and
from His bones (Eph. 5:30), all, I say, came from
the womb of Mary, being joined to the head, as it
were, in the manner of a body. *Hence, in this spiritual and mystical manner we are called the sons of
Mary and she is the Mother of us all.* Since, then, the

most Blessed Virgin is both the Mother of God and of man, *can anyone doubt that she ever strives with all her power and influence to move Christ, the head of the body of the Church* (Col. 1:18), *to bestow upon us, His members, His bounteous gifts,* first and foremost of which is that we may know Him and that we may live through Him (I John 4:9)?" (*Ad diem illum,* Feb. 2, 1904).

In brief, it was by her fiat that the Virgin of Nazareth entered upon her destiny of mother, Mother of God and of men.

VIII. THE DIVINE MOTHERHOOD AND THE HYPOSTATIC ORDER

The dogma of the divine motherhood presents a formidable problem to the human mind. While not intending to do away with the mystery it entails, we may nevertheless seek to investigate through reason what made it possible and what it involves. The best comparison to help us understand this deep mystery, at least in some small measure, is to be found in the generation of a human being. In that process the parents furnish the substance of the body, whereas God alone creates the soul and unites it with the body. From this union of body and soul results a human person.

Similarly, in order to be the Mother of God in the strict sense of the word and in all truth, it was not necessary that Mary be the author of the divine nature of the Word or even of His human soul. It was enough that she, like any other mother, be a true efficient cause of the body, specifically of the body of Jesus, thereby making it ready to be united with the soul of Christ and with the Person of the Word.

Thus, at the moment when in the usual course of events the conception of the Word Incarnate would have been accomplished, the eternal Person of the Son of God was at hand to terminate, miraculously and substitutionally, the movement of this act of conception. At that indivisible moment the following effects were brought about, simultaneously: 1   the creation of the human soul of Jesus;   2   its union with the body furnished by the Virgin Mary (this being the substantial union found in every human nature);   3   the union of the soul and the body with the Person of the Word (this being the hypostatic union);   4   the communicating of the uncreated existence of the Word to the human nature of Christ.

Thus the generative action of Mary is terminated simultaneously with, and in a manner intrinsically related to, both unions, that is, the union between the body and soul of Christ and the hypostatic union between the two natures, the divine and the human; and her generative action is also intrinsically related to, and terminated with, the subsistence of both natures in the uncreated existence of the Word, thereby reaching to the very limits of the Deity: *"attigit ad fines Deitatis"* (Cajetan, in II-II, Q. 3, art. 4). On this point we recommend highly the masterful study of Father M. J. Nicolas, O.P., "Le concept intégral de la maternité divine," in *Rev. Th.*, Vol. XLII, 1937, pp. 245ff.

IX.   MARY'S PARTICIPATION IN THE MYS-
TERY OF THE REDEMPTION

This is the critical point in present-day Mariology. We do not propose here to analyze and discuss the various stands taken on the matter. For a discussion of the question we suggest the work of Father Clément Dillenschneider, *Marie au service de la rédemption,* published in 1947. In our opinion, this is both the most complete and the most reliable study on the question.

In addition, we quote here some pontifical texts on which we have based our own thought and opinion regarding the matter under consideration. To be sure, the magisterium of the Church has not yet taken an explicit stand on the question of Mary's coredemptive role insofar as it pertains to the *acquisition* of all graces of salvation. However, theological development of the question is steadily going on, and it seems to us that the mind of the Church is moving in the direction of affirming Mary's participation, not only in the distribution of all graces but also in the acquisition of all graces, with the definite proviso that we be always careful to note that the coredemptive action of Mary is completely and totally subordinate to, and dependent on, the unique mediation and the universal redemption of Christ.

1 Regarding the *community of sufferings:* "The Mother of God merits praise and glory not merely because when God the only-begotten Son was to be born of a human being, she provided Him the substance of His flesh by which He could become the sacrificial victim for the salvation of men; but also because she performed the office of watching over and fostering this same victim, and in due time even presented Him to the altar of sacrifice. *Hence the reason why the Mother and the Son are never dissociated in their life and labors,* so that the words of the prophet are equally true of both, namely: 'My life is wasted with grief, and my years in sighs' (Ps. 30:11). Indeed, when His last hour had come, the Mother of

Jesus stood at the foot of the Cross, not simply witnessing the cruel spectacle, but *rejoicing in her heart* that her only-born Son was being offered for the salvation of mankind; and so great, moreover, was her co-suffering with Him that, had it been possible, she would have preferred to undergo in herself all the torments suffered by her Son" (Pius X, *Ad diem illum*, Feb. 2, 1904).

2 Regarding the *community of expiation*: "Whether we consider the fact that she offered herself as a handmaid to the Lord for the office of motherhood, or the fact that together with her Son she consecrated herself to Him in the Temple, in any event *it was by reason of both actions that Mary at this time in her life was already His partner and associate in the arduous work of expiation for mankind.* For this reason also it cannot be doubted that in her own soul she suffered with Him, in the highest possible degree, all the exceeding anguish and the most painful torments of her Son. Besides, it was most fitting that this divine sacrifice be offered with her present and looking on, since she had so magnanimously fostered and nourished the victim for it. And this is as it happened at the end, when this same mystery was brought to its sorrowful accomplishment. Mary His Mother stood by the Cross of Jesus; moved by her great love and desire to receive us as her children, *she voluntarily offered her Son in satisfaction of divine justice, dying with Him in spirit, her heart pierced by the sword of sorrow*" (Leo XIII, *Iucunda semper*, Sept. 6, 1894).

3 Regarding the *community of merits*: "Because she surpassed all others in holiness and in closeness to Christ, and because she was chosen by Him to be

His associate in the work of saving mankind, *Mary merits for us congruently, as is said, what Christ merited condignly"* (Pius X, *Ad diem illum*, Feb. 2, 1904).

4 Regarding the *community of sacrifice:* "No one will die an everlasting death who has the most Blessed Virgin at his side, especially in his last hour. This opinion of the doctors of the Church, which agrees with the sentiment of the Christian people and which, moreover, is continually confirmed by experience, rests above all on the fact that *the sorrowful Virgin shared in Christ's work of redemption;* and having been chosen to be the *Mother of men,* with joyous heart she received the children entrusted to her by testament of divine love, as it were, and exercises most loving care over them" (Pius XI, *Explorata res,* Feb. 2, 1923).

5 Regarding the *title of Coredemptress:* "She suffered with her suffering and dying Son, and almost died with Him; and for the salvation of men she surrendered her rights and privileges of mother over her Son and, so far as it pertained to her, sacrificed her Son to placate the justice of God—all this in such a manner that it can truly be said *that together with Christ she redeemed the human race"* (Benedict XV, *Inter Sodalicia,* March 22, 1918).

"O Mother of love and mercy, thou who as Coredemptress wast filled with compassion as thou stoodst at the side of thy most dearly beloved Son when, on the altar of the Cross, He wrought the redemption of mankind . . . conserve and increase in us each day the precious fruits of the redemption and of thy compassion" (Pius XI, *Osservatore Romano,* April 29-30, 1935).

The preceding quotation is from an address delivered on the radio by Pope Pius XI at the end of the jubilee year that had been proclaimed to commemorate the nineteen hundredth anniversary of the Redemption. It was addressed to a large assembly of bishops, prelates, and faithful gathered about the grounds of the grotto of Massabielle.

6   Regarding the causal connection between the two aspects of *acquisition* and *distribution* of all graces: "Hence the reason why the Mother and the Son are never dissociated in their life and labors, so that the words of the prophet are equally true of both, namely: 'My life is wasted with grief, and my years in sighs' (Ps. 30:11). By reason of this community of sorrow and will between Mary and Christ, *she merited to become in a most worthy manner the restorer of the world, and thereby the distributress of all blessings* that Jesus through His blood and death acquired for us" (Pius X, *Ad diem illum,* Feb. 2, 1904).

X.   THE PREDESTINATION OF MARY

The particular destiny that God assigns to any being gives us the clue to the explanation of its nature, as well as the clue to its place in the divine plan. Thus, the predestination decreed for Mary gives us the greatest possible insight, vouchsafed by the wisdom of God Himself, into the mystery of her divine motherhood. This mystery constitutes the highest ground of all her privileges both in the order of nature and in the order of grace and glory; for it is by reason of this mystery that Mary is affiliated with the hypostatic order in an intrinsic manner, so as to touch at its very essence. Hence, as on the one hand the ultimate reason for the Incarnation cannot be fully resolved except in the higher light of Christ's predestination, so on the other hand it is the understanding of Mary's predestination that permits us to grasp the ground and reason of her divine motherhood. Moreover, what is to the point here is that, according to the Bull *Ineffabilis,* the Mother and the Son are united and brought together in partnership by one and the same decree of predestination ("uno eodemque decreto").

Doubtless, the angels and mankind were also included in this same decree of predestination whereby God established the present plan of the universe; but their association with the hypostatic order is effected in a manner that does not join them intrinsically and essentially with that order, since they are united with it only by the unity of order. Mary, on the other hand, is affiliated with the hypostatic order, not indeed by a substantial union and with her whole person, like Christ, but by the term and end result toward which her divine motherhood of its very nature tended, a term that gives her a relationship with the Person of Christ that is intrinsically, or essentially, reciprocal. This divine motherhood, moreover, committed her to the coredemption of the world.

In this connection Leo XIII wrote as follows: "Having no part in original sin, the Virgin, being chosen the Mother of God, by this very fact was made to share in the work of saving mankind, and for this reason she enjoys such grace and power with her Son that no other human or angelic being ever possessed or can possess greater power and grace" (*Supremi Apostolatus,* Sept. 1, 1883).

Pope Pius IX came back to this same thought and made it even more explicit when he said: "For this was she chosen the Mother of Christ, that she might be His partner and associate in redeeming mankind" (*Auspicatus profecto, A.A.S.,* Vol. XXV, 1833, p. 80).

XI. THE ROSARY, THE EMBODIMENT OF DEVOTION TO MARY

The rosary has an essential place in Catholic piety and devotion. Pope Leo XIII made it the subject of not fewer than twenty-two letters and decrees, forming a rich source of doctrinal teaching on Mary. He spoke of the rosary as the "epitome of the cult due to her" (Encyclical *Octobri mense,* Sept. 22, 1891).

In praying the rosary the whole man is engaged; both his body and his mind are occupied. While with his lips he whispers or recites the Hail Marys, in his soul he meditates on God. As he goes from decade to decade he ponders over all the various mysteries of Christianity. Thus, through earnest meditation on the mysteries, the soul of man may rise to the highest levels of contemplation, for in so doing he will be reminded of the blessings wrought by God through the Incarnation and Redemption; his spiritual view will open to the bright vistas of the state of glory; and, equally important, he will find in the rosary the most perfect models of holiness to follow in his life on earth.

Hence, devotion to the rosary, which is both so wonderfully human and so wholly divine, meets perfectly the requirements of a spiritual and mystical life based on the Incarnation. It is in fact, according to the teaching of Leo XIII, the great prayer of the Church to Mary the Mediatress.

Achaz, King of Juda, reign, 21

Ain-Karem. *See* 'Ain-Karim (Carem)

'Ain-Karim (Carem) 16, 39

Albert the Great, St. *See* Albertus Magnus, St.

Albertus Magnus, St., on the compassion of Mary, 110, 110n

"Almah," 22

Ambrose, St., quoted on spiritual life in Mary, 121n

Annunciation. *See* Mary, Blessed Virgin, Annunciation

Anselm, St., quoted on divine motherhood of Mary, 108

Apostles, aided by Blessed Virgin Mary, 70-71

Ascension, of Christ. *See* Jesus Christ, Ascension

Assumption of the Blessed Virgin Mary. *See* Mary, Blessed Virgin, Assumption

Atonement, for sins
Christ's part in, 51-53, 60-61
Mary's part in, 51-56, 84

Augustine, St. *See* Augustinus, Aurelius, St., Bp. of Hippo

Augustinus, Aurelius, St., Bp. of Hippo, on the Blessed Virgin, 24

Axioms, Marian, 7, 134-136

Beatific vision, enjoyed by Christ on earth, 91, 92

Benedict XV, Pope, *Inter Sodalicia,* 147

Bernard, St.
on the pre-eminence and transcendence of the Blessed Virgin, 135-136
quoted on the Incarnation, 141

Bernardine of Siena, St. *See* Bernardino da Siena, St.

Bernardino da Siena, St., on grace, 99n

Blessed Trinity. *See* Trinity

Caesar Augustus, decree of, 42

Cana, wedding at, 47-48

Canticle of Canticles, 104

Cenacle, 69

Christianity, Mary's place in, 12-13

Church
aided by Mary, 70-72
regard of Mary, 101-115

Conformity with Christ, Marian axiom of, 135

Coredemptress, of the world, 5, 7-9, 13-15, 18, 53-55, 64-67, 77, 83-84, 147-148
according to Sacred Scripture, 13-15

Cornelius a Lapide. *See* Lapide, Cornelius à

Council of Ephesus. *See* Ephesus, Council of

Dillenschneider, Clement, *Marie au service de la rédemption,* 145

Divine revelation. *See* Revelation, divine

Elect, the, source of happiness for, 4-5

Elizabeth, Mary's visit to, 38-40

Ephesus, Council of, 8

Eucharist, participation in by first Christians, 71

Eve, new, 15-17, 54, 101-102, 136-137

Expiation, for mankind, Mary's part, 146-147

Fittingness, Marian axiom of, 134-135

Florilegium mariale, 131

Grace(s)
acquisition of, Mary's part in, 49-50, 145, 148
distribution of, Mary's part in, 5, 49-50, 72-78, 94, 98-100, 145, 148
See also Merit

Holy Eucharist. *See* Eucharist

Holy Ghost. *See* Holy Spirit

Holy Spirit, Mary guided by, 89, 90

Human nature, failings of, Mary preserved from, 88-89

Immaculate Conception. *See* Mary, Blessed Virgin, Immaculate Conception

Incarnation, importance of, 140-141

Ineffabilis Deus. *See* Pius IX, Pope

Intercession, Mary's power of, 5

Isaias, prophet
on the birth of Christ, 22
on the Blessed Virgin, 21
prophecy of, 50
vision of, 21

Jansenism, 8

Jesus Christ
as King, 78-79
Ascension, 69
birth, 42-43
early life, 45-47
enjoyment of beatific vision on earth, 91, 92
Mary as co-worker with, 15-17, 18
Mediator for world, 73-74
Passion of, source of holiness, 57
place in the universe, 3-4, 81-83
priest and king of His Church, 75-76
Resurrection, 68
saviour of mankind, 62-63

Joannes of Damascus, St., regarding divine motherhood of Mary, 107-108

John Damascene, St. *See* Joannes of Damascus, St.

Joseph, St.
angel's message to, 41-42
holiness of, 46n
mission of, 46n

Keuppens, J., *Mariologiae compendium*, 131

Knowledge, Mary's gift of, 91-94

Lapide, Cornelius à
on the divine motherhood, 129-130
on the pre-eminence and transcendence of the Blessed Virgin, 136

Lawrence of Brindisi, St., on Marian axiom of conformity with Christ, 135

Leo XIII, Pope
Iucunda semper, 146-147
Octobri mense, 150
quoted on dignity of Mary, 107
quoted on Mary as Coredemptress, 150
quoted on Mary as dispenser of graces, 113n
quoted on Mary as repository of graces, 113
quoted on the Rosary, 150, 151
Supremi Apostolatus, 150

Life, spiritual. *See* Spiritual life

Magnificat, 39-40

Malachias, prophet, prophecy of, 34

Marian axioms. *See* Axioms, Marian

Mariology, scientific order for, 132-134

Mary, Blessed Virgin
adviser to Apostles, 70
Annunciation, 34-37
as "the complement of the Trinity," 85n
Assumption, 72, 97-98
characteristics, 23-24, 27-28, 47
compassion of, 109-112
Coredemptress of world, 5, 7-9, 13-15, 18, 53-55, 64-67, 77, 83-84, 147-148
death, 96-97
destiny, 49
devotion to, 113-115, 120-125
traits of, 8-9

directed by Holy Spirit, 27

distributor of graces, 5, 49-50, 72-78, 94, 98-100, 145, 148

divine motherhood, 3-11, 6-7, 17-18, 86, 87, 106-109, 117-120, 129-132, 143-144, 148-150

early life, 31-33

grace and holiness of, 25-27, 138-140

Immaculate Conception, 5, 20-30, 54-55

dogma of, 8, 26, 137-138

intercessor for world, 74-75

life at Nazareth, 45-47

mediatress for world, 9, 51, 119-120

mediatress in Heaven, 98-100

mediatress of grace, 76-78

merits gained for all, 72

Mother of Jesus, 37-39, 55-56

Mother of the world, 17-18, 116-120

new Eve, 15-17, 54, 101-102, 136-137

part in the Redemption, 110-112, 145-148

passion of, 49-67

place in supernatural order, 25, 26, 123

place in the universe, 3-4, 25

possessor of grace, 87-90

power of intercession, 5

predestination of, 148-150

preserved from sin, 22-25

Purification, 44

purity of, 104-106

Queen of Heaven, 112-113

religious life, 31-33

role in Christ's kingship, 79-80

sacrifice on Calvary, 61-62

sanctifying grace in, 26

source of all grace, 57-59

spiritual growth of, 29-30

symbols of, in Sacred Scripture, 102-104

without sin, 95n

See also Mariology

Mediatress, of the world, Mary's mission of, 9, 51, 119-120

Merit, for mankind, Mary's part, 147

Merkelbach, Benoit Henri, on the divine motherhood, 130-131

Messianic prophecy, Mary in, 14, 16, 21, 22

Micheas, prophet, prophecy of, 42

Motherhood

coredemptive, 6-7

divine

role of, 3-11, 6-7, 17-18, 86, 87, 106-109, 117-120, 148-150

and the hypostatic order, 143-144

in Marian theology, 129-132

Nathanael, 48

Nescience, 89n

Nicholas, M.J., *Le concept intégral de la maternité divine*, 144

Order

hypostatic, 149-150

supernatural, Mary's place in, 148-150

Paul, St.

quoted on Christ's mission, 52

quoted on spiritual life in Mary, 121n

Pentecost, feast of, 70

Pius IX, Pope

Auspicatus profecto, 150

Ineffablis Deus, 149

quoted on grace and holiness of Mary, 138-140

on the Immaculate Conception, 26, 137

quoted on Mary as Coredemptress, 150

Pius X, Pope

Ad diem illum, 141-143, 146, 147, 148

on Marian axiom of fittingness, 64n-65n
on the Incarnation, 141-143
Pius XI, Pope
    Explorata res, 147
    Lux Veritatis, 129-130, 136
    on the divine motherhood,
    129-130
    quoted on dignity of Mary,
    107
    quoted on Mary as Coredemp-
    tress, 148
Power, intercessory, with God,
29
Pre-eminence and transcend-
ence, Marian axiom of,
135-136
Protestantism, 8
Purification of the Blessed Vir-
gin Mary. *See* Mary,
Blessed Virgin, Purifica-
tion
Redemption, Mary's participa-
tion in, 12-13, 18, 110-
112, 145-148
Resurrection of Christ. *See* Jesus
Christ, Resurrection
Revelation, divine, 10
Rosary, place in Catholic devo-
tion, 150-151
Sacrifice, Mary's part in, 147
Sapiential Books, The, 104

Shema, 32
Simeon, prophecy of, 44-45
Sin, malice of, 52-53
Sorrowful Mother, devotion to,
109
Spiritual life, center of, 121
Suarez, Francisco, S.J., on the
divine motherhood, 130
Suffering
    Mary's part in Christ's, 145-
    146
    Mary's part of, 95-96
Theotokos, 8, 106
Thérèse, St., quoted on the
Holy Family, 9
Thomas Aquinas, St.
    on divine motherhood of
    Mary, 107, 129
    on required grace, 134-135
    on the pre-eminence and
    transcendence of the
    Blessed Virgin, 136
Tota mater, 17
Trinity, place in the universe, 3
Union, hypostatic, 144
Veneration, to Mary, 5-6
Verlaine, Paul Marie, 115
Water into wine, miracle of, 48
World
    Mother of the, 17-18
    redemption of, by Christ, 60
Zachary, message of angel to, 34

DATE DUE

DE 14 '84			
NO 12 '88			
MAY 0 1 98			
MAR 2 '00			
GAYLORD			PRINTED IN U.S.A